TIBET

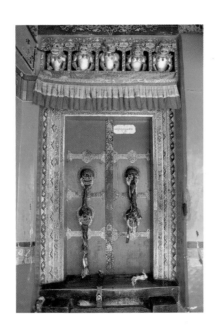

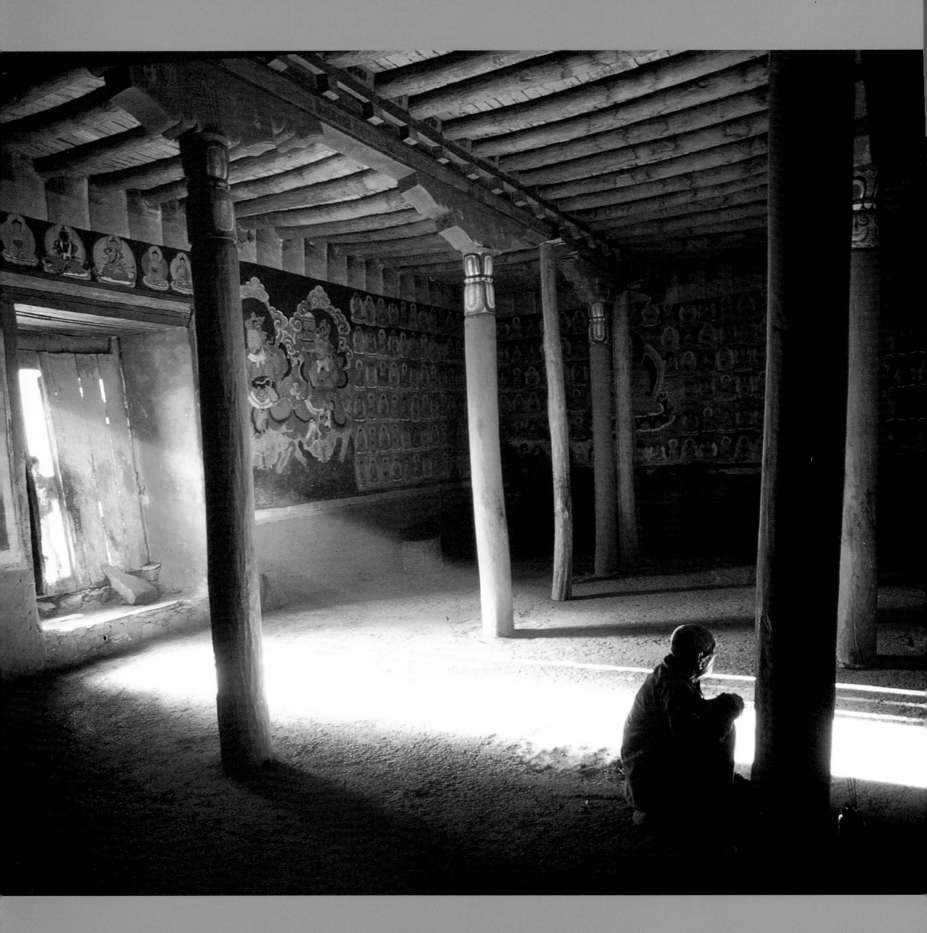

TIBET

Life, Myth, and Art

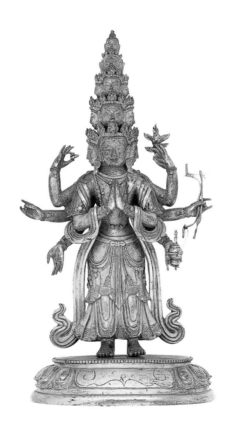

MICHAEL WILLIS

Thorsons
Directions for Life

Thorsons
An imprint of HarperCollins*Publishers*
77–85 Fulham Palace Road
Hammersmith, London, England W6 8JB

Published in the United States by Thorsons in 2003

Published in 1999 by Stewart, Tabori and Chang
A division of U.S. Media Holdings, Inc.
115 West 18th Street, New York, NY 10011

Created, conceived, and designed by
Duncan Baird Publishers
Sixth Floor
Castle House
75–76 Wells Street
London W1T 3QH

Project editor: *Peter Bently*
Editor: *Joanne Levêque*
Designer: *Gail Jones*
Picture researcher: *Julia Ruxton*
Calligraphy: *Susanne Haines*
Commissioned illustrations: *Sally Taylor (artistpartners ltd)*
Decorative borders: *Iona McGlashan*
Map artworks: *Celia Hart*

Library of Congress Cataloging-in-Publication Data is available.

1 3 5 7 9 10 8 6 4 2

ISBN: 0-00-766873-2

Typeset in Perpetua and Bernhard Modern
Color reproduction by Colourscan, Singapore
Printed and bound in Singapore

NOTE
The abbreviations CE and BCE are used throughout this book:
CE Common Era (the equivalent of AD)
BCE Before the Common Era (the equivalent of BC)

HALF TITLE **An elaborately decorated doorway at the Potala Palace in Lhasa.**

FRONTISPIECE **Dusk at the Tibetan Leh monastery in Ladakh, northern India.**

TITLE **Gilded bronze, 19th-century figure representing Avalokiteshvara, the patron deity of Tibet, in his multiheaded form.**

PAGE 6 **His Holiness the Dalai Lama and monks of the Gelug-pa order performing a Buddhist ceremony at Dharamsala, northern India.**

CONTENTS

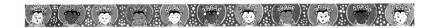

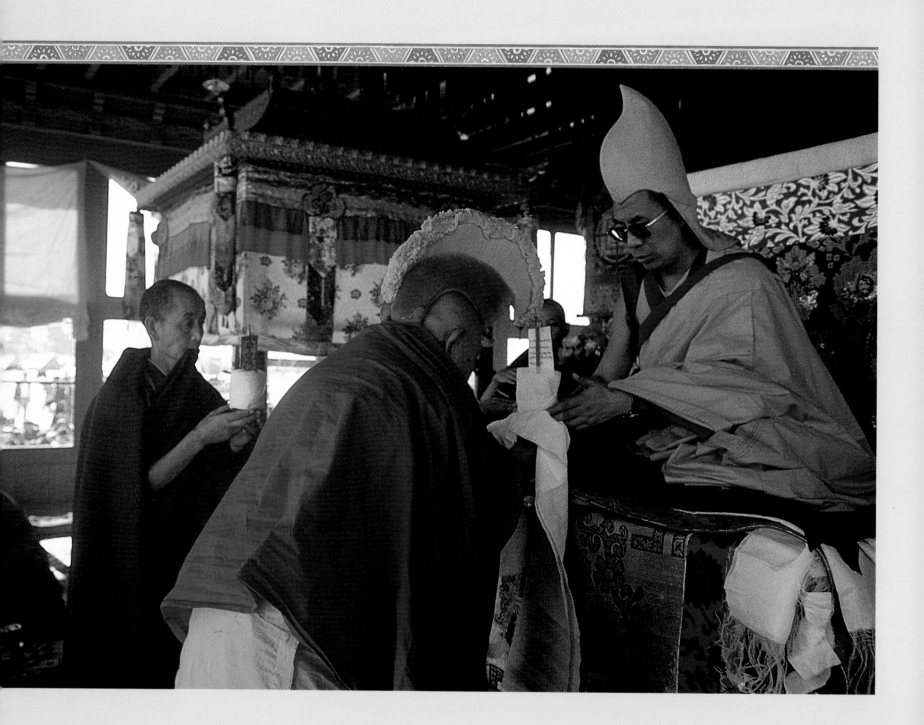

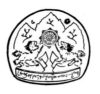

THE DALAI LAMA

FOREWORD

Tibet is home to a rich and ancient culture that has been subject to many formative influences. Among these our natural environment has fostered a strong spirit of freedom and resilience in the Tibetan character.

Of course, when we think of Tibetan culture, we think of Buddhism because of the profound effect that it has had on the Tibetan way of life. Every culture has its distinguishing characteristics and Tibetans have long emphasised the development of such inner values as compassion and wisdom. We regard such qualities as the most important treasures a human being can collect in his or her lifetime. This is the true wealth, which benefits others and ourselves in the short and long term, that is symbolised in our paintings, statues and ritual implements.

Tibetan civilisation forms a distinct part of the world's precious common heritage. Humanity would be the poorer if it were to be lost. I am sure that people reading this book, and enjoying the photographs it contains, will come to a better and more sympathetic understanding of the Tibetan people and their traditions and perhaps be inspired to support our efforts to save Tibetan culture from disappearing forever.

March 3, 1999

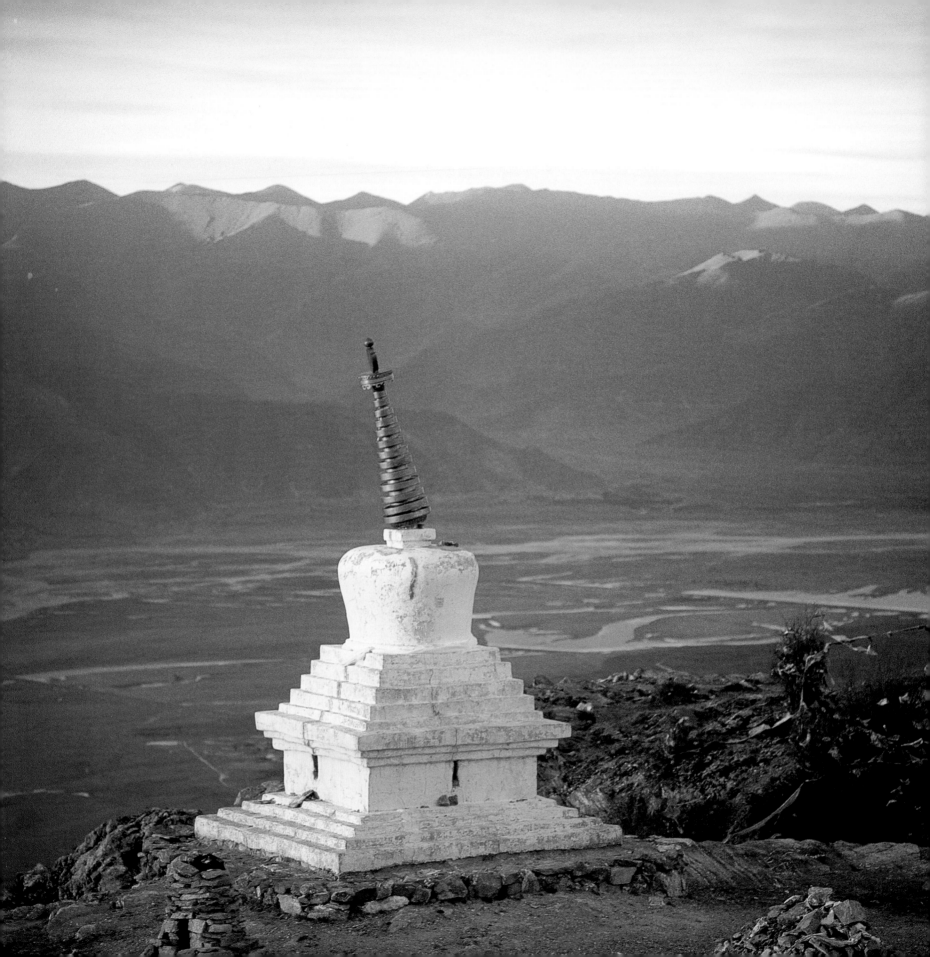

IMAGE AND IMAGINATION

"This center of heaven/This core of earth/This heart of the World/Fenced round by snowy mountains/The headland of all rivers/Where peaks are high and the land is pure/A country so good/Where men are born as sages and heroes/And act according to good laws." This poetic description of Tibet, written in the ninth century CE, gives rapturous expression to the defining features of Tibetan civilization: the "good laws" of Buddhism and the high peaks of the Himalayas. Protected by the world's tallest mountains and drawing only what they needed from the neighboring civilizations of India and China, the Tibetans developed a unique society, philosophy, and art which have long inspired fascination and deep respect.

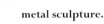

THE SOUL OF TIBET

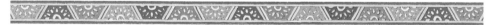

Although Tibet is a predominantly Buddhist country, Buddhism was only established there in the seventh century CE—more than one thousand years after the time of the Buddha. Born Siddhartha Gautama in the sixth century BCE, the Buddha was a north Indian prince who renounced the privileges of royal life to seek the Truth as a wandering ascetic. The places of his birth (Lumbini), enlightenment (Bodh Gaya), first sermon (Sarnath), and final passing (Kusinagara) became important centers of pilgrimage and were later among the sites visited by Tibetans in search of the Buddha's teachings, or *dharma* (see map on page 17).

The fundamental principles of the Buddha's *dharma* are known as the "Four Noble Truths" and their startling simplicity and profundity may account for the appeal of the Buddhist approach to life to Tibetans and others. The Noble Truths are: all beings inevitably endure suffering (*duhkha*); the cause (*samudaya*) of suffering is desire; the cause of desire can be contained (*nirodha*); and to contain the cause of desire one must follow the Buddha's path (*marga*).

The entire philosophical, religious, social, and artistic edifice of the Buddhist civilization of Tibet is built on these four principles. They explain why Buddhism is not simply a school of philosophy, but a practical undertaking that aims to revolutionize human life by putting seekers on the path to enlightenment (*nirvana*, literally "without desire"). Enlightenment is a unique mental state characterized by complete nonattachment to the material world. As Buddhists would say, *nirvana* is neither fullness nor emptiness, being nor nonbeing, substance nor nonsubstance.

Attaining this state of indescribable freedom requires application—the seeker

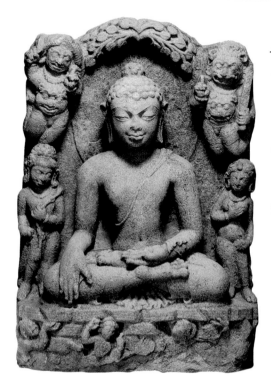

ABOVE **This Indian sandstone stela dates from the late seventh century CE, the period when Buddhism was first introduced into Tibet from India. The Buddha is shown touching the ground with one hand, the traditional gesture of calling the earth to witness his enlightenment.**

RIGHT **A large solitary figure of the Buddha with halos around his head and body features in the center of this *thangka* (Tibetan painting on cloth). The miniature scenes in the landscape are Jataka ("Birth") stories, which illustrate how the Buddha, through the practice of virtue, perfected himself over many lifetimes. The scenes are identified by labels written in Tibetan; on the bottom is an inscription of the Chinese emperor Wanli (1573–1620), who was an important patron of Tibetan Buddhism.**

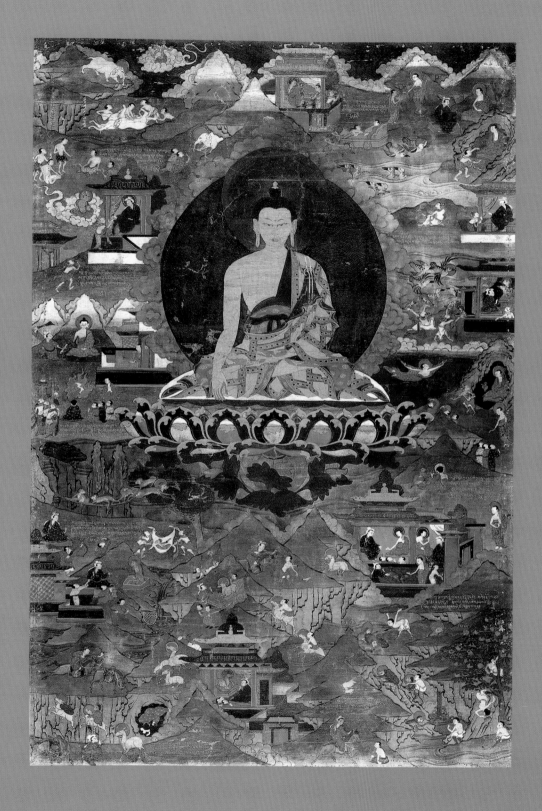

needs a lifestyle and environment that are conducive to purity of word, thought, and deed. These requirements led directly to the institution of monasticism, a key feature of Buddhism in Tibet and elsewhere.

Both during and after the Buddha's lifetime, a number of monks attained enlightenment. They were known as the Arhats, or "Worthy Ones." Little moved by the suffering of others, the Arhats had no inclination to teach the *dharma* beyond affirming by example that the Buddha's path provided the way to *nirvana*. For this reason some Buddhist thinkers regarded the Arhats as incomplete, in that they lacked the profound compassion that inspired the Buddha to teach the *dharma* for the good of all humankind.

Such compassion is a key feature of the Buddhist schools—which include those of Tibet—known collectively as Mahayana (the "Great Vehicle"). Compassion is embodied in the divine figures known as Bodhisattvas, literally "Those whose Essence is Supreme Knowledge." In the Mahayana view, the Bodhisattvas supersede the Arhats because they stand on the verge of enlightenment, but delay their final attainment of *nirvana* out of compassion for suffering beings, in order that they may assist others to achieve liberation. Tibetans have always followed the Mahayana traditions and consequently Bodhisattvas are widely venerated throughout the country. The Bodhisattva Avalokiteshvara, the Supreme Lord of Compassion, became the patron deity of Tibet—incarnated in the person of the Dalai Lama, the Tibetan priest-king.

According to Mahayana, all individuals are potentially Bodhisattvas, but this sublime state can be achieved only by the diligent cultivation of virtue over hun-

ABOVE This bronze figure shows a fierce Bon deity trampling on two Buddhas (rather than the demons often shown under the feet of many Buddhist deities). He holds a figure of Garuda—the eagle-like creature known for his destruction of poisonous snakes—and a thunderbolt (*vajra*), an emblem usually held by Vajra Pani, a protective Bodhisattva.

dreds of lifetimes. In contrast, Vajrayana (the "Vehicle of the Diamantine Thunderbolt") asserts that there is a "rapid path." The Great Adepts (*Mahasiddha*s) followed this path and attained enlightenment immediately by using special techniques and rituals. These powerful practices—developed by the Great Adepts or revealed to them by compassionate deities—are collectively known as Tantra (see page 105).

When the first Buddhist missionaries and masters of Tantra ventured into Tibet, they faced a royal cult strikingly similar to that of ancient India. Violent animal sacrifices, controlled by a priestly elite, were deemed necessary to maintain order in the heavens and to win favor from the gods. Just as the Buddha had effectively challenged the sacrificial culture of India, so the early Buddhists in Tibet were able to displace established priests and rituals, transforming powerful local deities into protectors of the *dharma* (see page 122).

What survived of Tibet's pre-Buddhist cults was reorganized into Bon, a religion which persists to this day, especially in neighboring Bhutan. Although distinct from Buddhism—and opposed to many of its tenets—Bon has a monastic organization, textual tradition, and pantheon of deities which are heavily influenced by the Tibetan Buddhist examples.

RIGHT **Avalokiteshvara, the Lord of Compassion, is represented by this 13th-century CE seated bronze figure. His generosity is shown by his open hand, which symbolizes the granting of wishes. The figure has turquoise inlays, a common feature of Tibetan metalwork.**

THE TSANGPO RIVER

The Tsangpo is one of Asia's mightiest rivers—it is more than 1,800 miles (2,900km) long from its source in western Tibet to its confluence with the Ganga River on the great alluvial plains of Bangladesh. The Tsangpo is also known as the Brahmaputra, literally the "Son of Brahma," because its source is traced by some to Lake Manasarovar, a body of water traditionally thought to have been created by the god Brahma for the pilgrims visiting Mount Kailas (see pages 48–49).

Known near its source as the Tachok Tsangpo and the Yarlung Tsangpo further downstream, the river flows eastward across the entire width of central Tibet, drawing water from innumerable mountain streams and tributaries. The Tsangpo is navigable for more than 370 miles (600km) from Lhartse, near Dingri. River journeys and crossings are made in flat-bottomed riverboats.

In ancient times the Tsangpo was an important highway for trade and pilgrimage within Tibet. However, in eastern Tibet, near the border with Assam, the river surges through the world's deepest gorges, plunging more than 9,800 feet (3,000m) in less than 28 miles (45km). This has meant that, although the Tsangpo helps account for the cultural unity of Tibet itself, it has never served as a channel of communication with India.

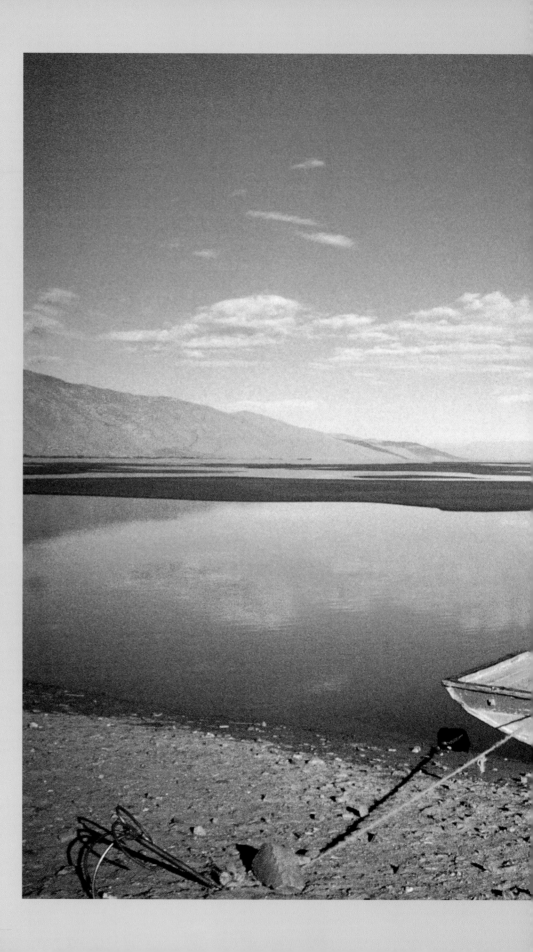

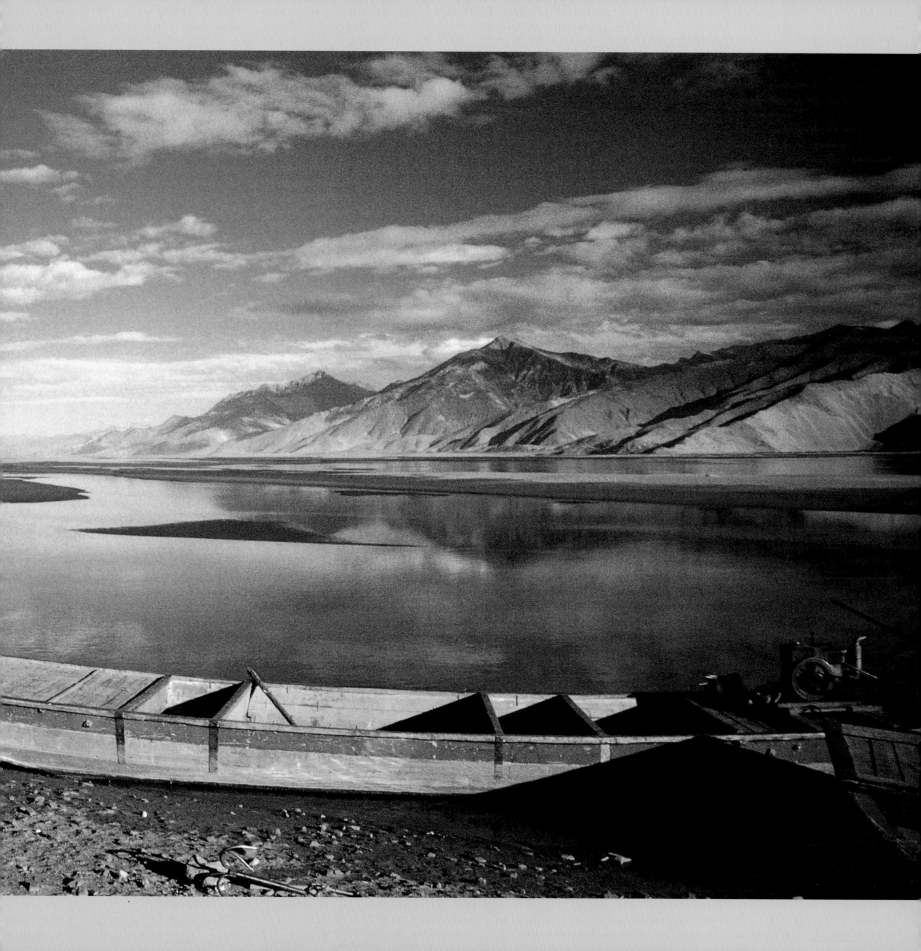

THE STORY OF TIBET

Tibet became a unified kingdom in the seventh century CE under King Song-tsen Gampo, a dynamic ruler who led his armies to the frontiers of China and India. Songtsen Gampo, whose forebears came from the Yarlung Valley, was not a practicing Buddhist, but his queens, from Nepal and China, built the first Buddhist temple in Lhasa and furnished it with images. However, Buddhism did not become firmly rooted until the following century, when King Trisong Detsen invited the Indian teacher Shantarakshita to establish Tibet's first Buddhist monastery, which he accomplished with the aid of the charismatic Padmasambhava (see page 32).

The Yarlung Empire disintegrated in the ninth century and Tibet became a dis-united collection of kingdoms and principalities. Interest in Buddhism remained limited until the tenth century, when Tibetans went to India to study and translate sacred texts. Indian masters also came to Tibet, the most celebrated being Atisha

RIGHT **The valley of Chongye became the burial ground of the Yarlung rulers and sixteen tumuli (mounds of earth) have been identified as the tombs of the greatest Tibetan kings, including Songsten Gampo. The adjacent Yarlung Valley, which gave its name to the dynasty that unified Tibet in the 7th century CE, has many temples, monasteries, caves, castles, and sacred peaks.**

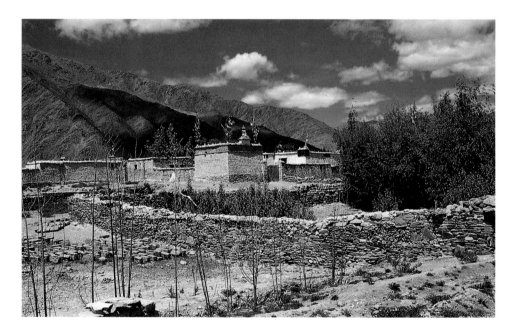

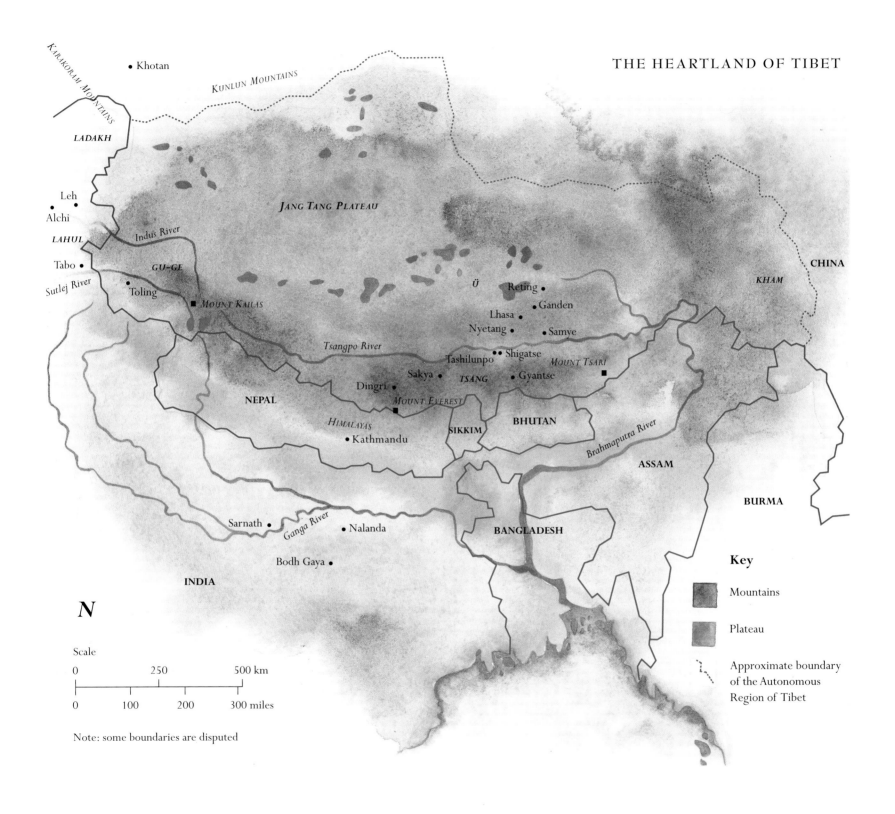

THE HEARTLAND OF TIBET

Khotan

KARAKORAM MOUNTAINS

KUNLUN MOUNTAINS

LADAKH

Leh

Alchi

LAHUL

Indus River

JANG TANG PLATEAU

CHINA

Tabo

GU~GE

KHAM

Sutlej River

Toling

MOUNT KAILAS

Ü

Reting

Ganden

Lhasa

Nyetang

Samye

Tsangpo River

Tashilunpo • Shigatse

MOUNT TSARI

Sakya *TSANG* Gyantse

Dingri

MOUNT EVEREST

NEPAL

BHUTAN

HIMALAYAS

SIKKIM

Kathmandu

Brahmaputra River

ASSAM

BANGLADESH

BURMA

Sarnath *Ganga River* Nalanda

Bodh Gaya

INDIA

N

Scale

0   250   500 km

0   100   200   300 miles

Note: some boundaries are disputed

Key

Mountains

Plateau

Approximate boundary
of the Autonomous
Region of Tibet

(see page 110), whose arrival in 1042 traditionally marks the "Second Propagation" of Buddhism in the country. Atisha's followers founded the Kadam-pa religious order, which stressed the importance of applying the ideals of a Bodhisattva in the practitioner's daily life.

Other orders founded around this time included the Sakya-pa, which won powerful allies and converts in the Mongol Empire, notably the emperor Kublai Khan (1215–1294). The collapse of the empire in the mid-fourteenth century ended Sakya-pa dominance and initiated an era of reevaluation and renewal within Tibet.

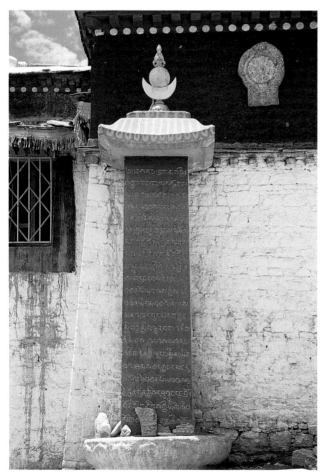

A new dynasty, the Pamotrupa, sought to revive the glory of the Yarlung kings, while the discovery of texts "hidden" by Padmasambhava gave fresh impetus to the Nyingma-pa order he had founded.

The most influential scholar and reformer of the time was Tsong Khapa (1357–1419). Inspired by Atisha, he advocated strict attention to monastic discipline. His teachings motivated his disciples to found the Gelug-pa, or "Yellow Hat," religious order. The Gelug-pa at first avoided direct involvement in secular matters, but their piety attracted Mongolian attention. In 1578 the Mongol leader Altan Khan gave a prominent Gelug-pa *lama* the title Dalai Lama. Half a century later, with Mongolian assistance, the Dalai Lama became Tibet's sacred and secular leader. This theocratic system of government survived until 1959, when the Communist Chinese drove the fourteenth Dalai Lama into exile.

LEFT **This tall stone slab, known as the Samye Doring, is located beside the main temple at Samye, the oldest Buddhist monastery in Tibet (see page 40). Dating to the 8th century CE, the slab is engraved with a long inscription proclaiming Buddhism as the state religion. Similar stelae can be found at Lhasa (see page 20).**

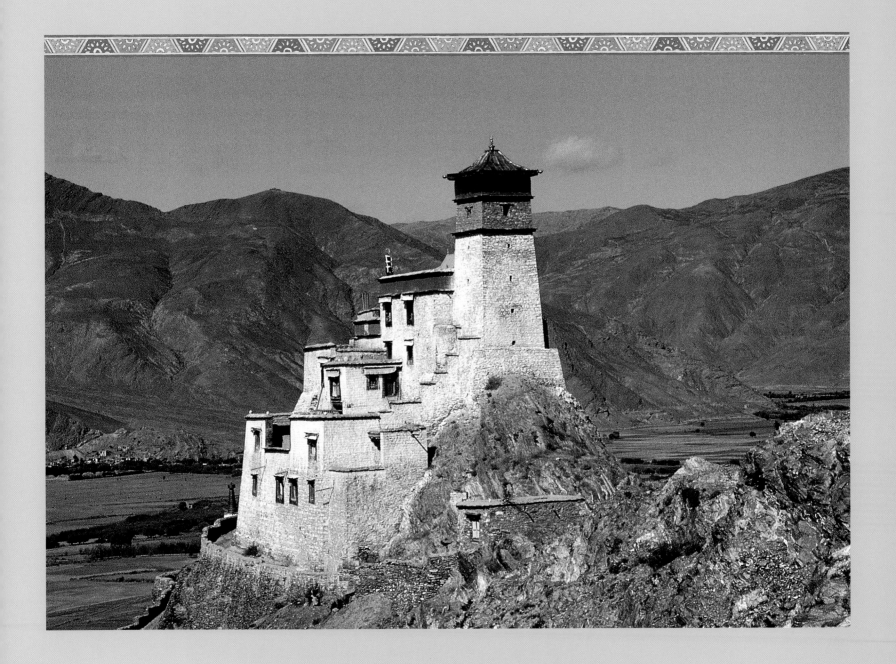

The Yumbu Lagang is said to be have been established by Nyatri Tsenpo, the first king of Tibet. The building has long ceased to be a fortified palace and has been rebuilt on several occasions, most recently beginning in 1982, following the Cultural Revolution. Chapels inside contain Buddha images and statues of historical figures, including the Yarlung kings and their ministers.

THE HOLY CITY: LHASA

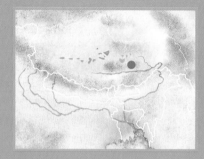

Lhasa is the capital of Tibet and its largest city. It is dominated by the Potala, the residence of the Dalai Lamas until 1959 when the Communist Chinese forced Tenzin Gyatso, the fourteenth Dalai Lama, into exile. This magnificent building was begun in 1645 shortly after Losang Gyatso, the fifth Dalai Lama—known as the "Great Fifth" on account of his wisdom, tolerance, and effectiveness as a ruler—came to power.

The Potala is named after Mount Potalaka, the celestial abode of Avalokiteshvara, the Bodhisattva of Compassion and patron deity of Tibet. Songsten Gampo, the king who built the first structure on the site in the seventh century CE, is regarded as an emanation of Avalokiteshvara, as is the "Great Fifth," under whom most of the present palace was constructed in the seventeenth century. Although an architectural project of unprecedented size and ambition, the Potala is built in the typical Tibetan style, with gently sloping walls and flat roofs resting

RIGHT Built in the 17th century CE, the Potala Palace towers over the capital city of Lhasa. The Potala served as a monastery and a fortress, as well as being the residence of the Dalai Lamas and the seat of the Tibetan government until 1959.

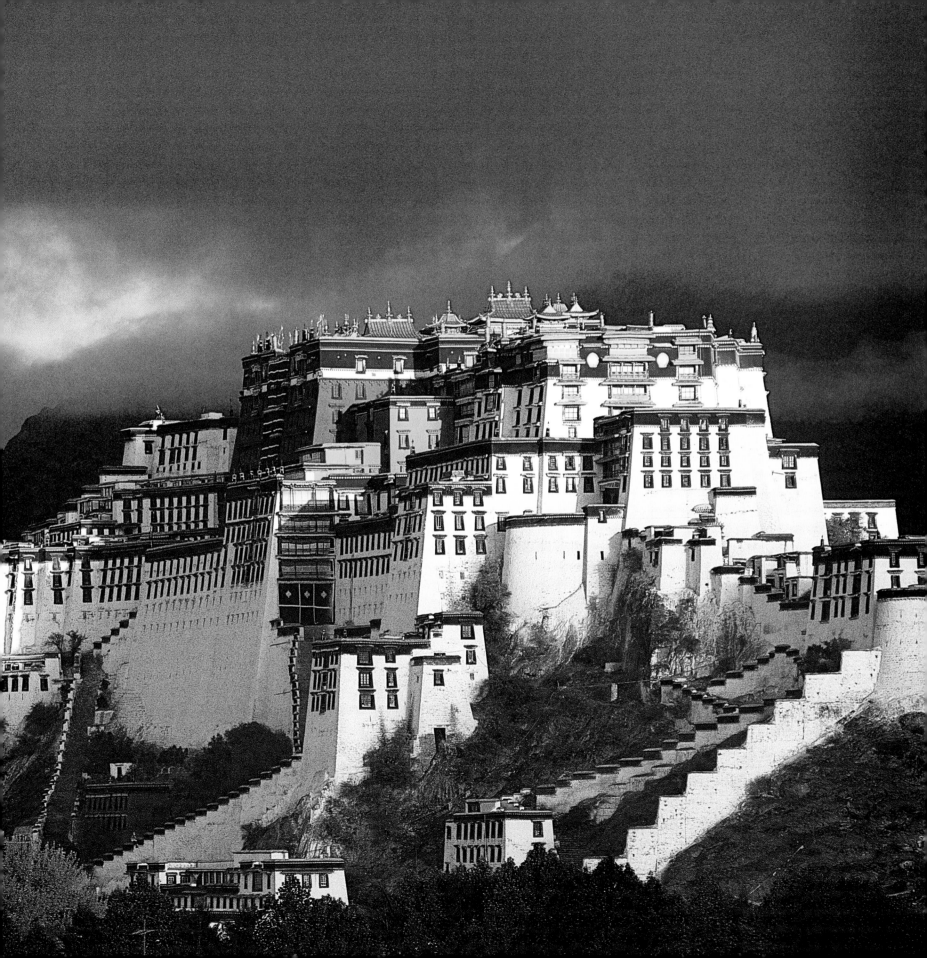

on wooden beams. The palace's curved gables reflect the influence of contemporary Chinese architecture.

The Potala's outer section is known as the "White Palace" and was the seat of government up to 1959. The lower walls of the White Palace are plain and were once used to display giant *thangka* paintings of the Buddhas during important festivals. Inside the White Palace are the winter apartments of the Dalai Lamas and a large three-storied hall known as the Tsom-chen Shar. It was here that the Dalai Lamas were enthroned and where envoys from China were received.

The upper section of the building, known as the "Red Palace," contains a series of temples, images, and shrines, including relics of the Dalai Lamas. This portion of the palace dates to the end of the seventeenth century and is attributed to Desi Sangye Gyatso, the regent who concealed the death of the fifth Dalai Lama so that the building could be completed. The Potala is a physical expression and potent emblem of the way in which Tibet was unified and ruled by the Dalai Lamas and the Gelug-pa order for three centuries.

Not far from the Potala is the Jo Khang, the "cathedral of Lhasa" and the most sacred temple in the whole of Tibet. It draws people from many parts of the country, especially at New Year when the dim passages of the building are crowded with pilgrims. Founded by Bhrikuti, Songsten Gampo's Nepalese queen, the Jo Khang has undergone frequent modification, repair, and restoration since it was first completed in 647CE.

The core of the building, a rectangular court surrounded by cells, follows the plan of Buddhist temples in India. On the eastern side of the court is a large chamber known as the Jowo Shakyamuni Lhakhang, which contains the famous sculpture of the Buddha known as Jowo Rinpoche. This image has a long history—it is

LEFT **One of the many elaborate roof decorations that embellish Lhasa's Potala Palace.**

reputed to have been made in India by Vishvakarma, the divine craftsman of the gods, and presented to China by an early Indian monarch. The details of this story suggest a distant memory of Ashoka, a great Indian king of the third century BCE who did much to further the spread of Buddhism.

In any event, the statue was brought to Tibet by Weng Cheng, Songsten Gampo's Chinese queen, and installed in the Jo Khang after the king's death in 650CE. It has remained there ever since and has been the subject of constant devotion and embellishment. The headdress was first added by the scholar Tsong Khapa (see page 18) and the precious outer robe was given by one of the Ming emperors.

BELOW The Potala can be seen in this view from the rooftops of the Jo Khang. The Jo Khang has often been refurbished over the centuries, one of the most recent additions being the gilt "Wheel of Dharma" shown here, which was added by the Mongol Ta Lama of Sera in 1927.

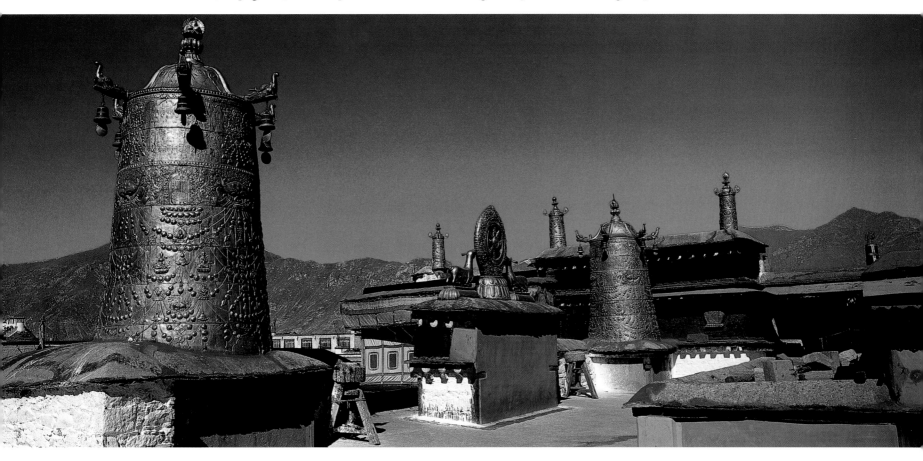

THE ART OF TIBET

Until very recent times, Tibetans viewed every aspect of life from a Buddhist standpoint—education, administration, landholding, and production were controlled or influenced by powerful *lamas* or monasteries. It was a world in which all boundaries between the temporal and spiritual spheres were erased, a world in which the Dalai Lama was at once the head of state and the supreme authority in spiritual matters. As a result, virtually all Tibetan art was religious in purpose.

Artists and craftspeople typically worked for monasteries and temples, their finest products finding a treasured place in shrines, chapels, and monastic libraries. Sculptures were carved and cast for worship; precious metals were hammered into lamps and incense burners for temple altars; masks were made for religious processions; and fine fabrics and embroideries—usually imported from India and China—were used to clothe images or to line the scroll paintings that play a key role in Tibetan devotional life. This religious artistic activity continues today, though on a reduced scale in Tibet itself since the depredations of the early period of Communist Chinese occupation.

Religious images play a very important role in Buddhism. Sculptures are not simply reminders of cosmic realities or mementos of the Buddha and the great teachers of the past. Rather, each sculpture is a living presence, an actual embodiment of what it represents. In Tibet and elsewhere, objects may be placed inside images in the course of their consecration in order to transform them from mundane raw materials—copper alloy in the case of most Tibetan sculpture—into living realities. Deposits in images vary enormously, but generally they include small scrolls with written or printed prayers and mystic diagrams relating to the deity or person depicted in the sculpture. One crucial element is a shaft or sliver of wood (*sogshing*), a "tree of life" that serves as the

LEFT **Butter lamps, made of brass or silver and shaped like goblets, are found on all Tibetan altars. The bowl is provided with a wick and filled with butter, which acts like candle wax.**

RIGHT **This sculpture of the saint Padmasambhava at Lhasa's Jo Khang temple is painted and draped with cloth, as is the custom with images which are actively under worship. Before the image is an altar lined with butter lamps and other ritual objects.**

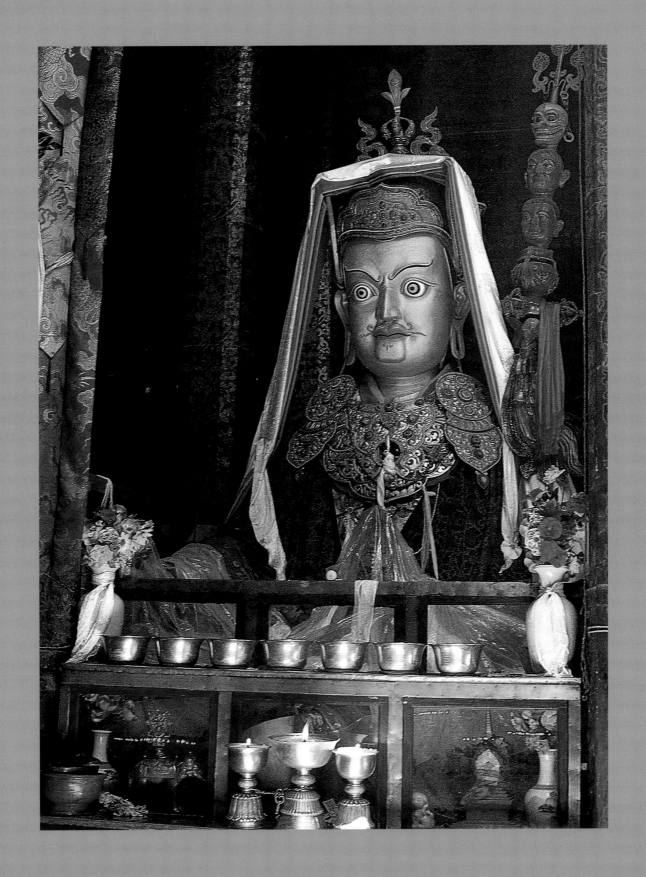

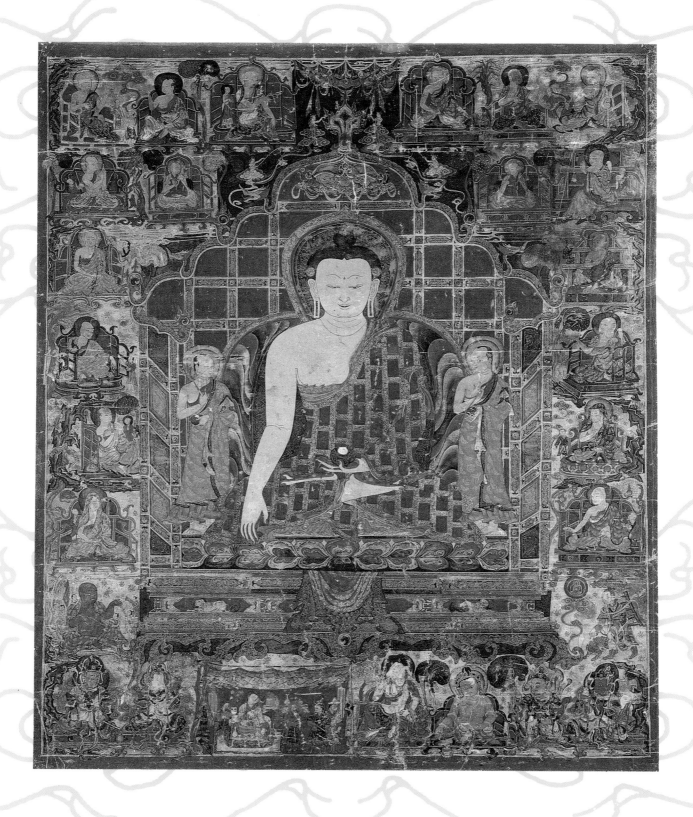

living "axis" of the sculpture. Images of historic individuals will also contain a relic relating directly to the deceased—often a small piece of ash collected after his or her cremation.

Once a sculpture has thus been "brought to life," it is treated like a living being. Images, as a result, are usually clothed, placed on a seat, and presented with food, water, and other gifts. Offering-cakes are made of butter and *tsampa* (roasted barley flour), but cakes of painted clay are also offered. A crucial part of worship is the lighting of butter lamps—there may be dozens of such lamps before the most important and popular sacred images.

Like sculptures, Tibetan paintings on cloth scrolls (*thangkas*) are not simply decorative. They depict deities, sacred beings, or saints and are brought to life by dedicatory prayers written on the reverse; sometimes the handprints of the *lama* who performed the dedication were added. *Thangka* paintings are hung inside chapels in accordance with the liturgical and ritual practices of the particular monastery or temple. The images they bear can serve a didactic purpose and the ordinary devotee may well worship them. Some *thangka*s may be viewed only by initiates as part of their mystical training.

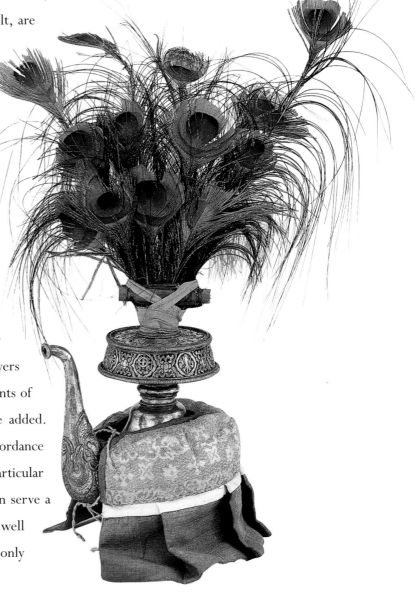

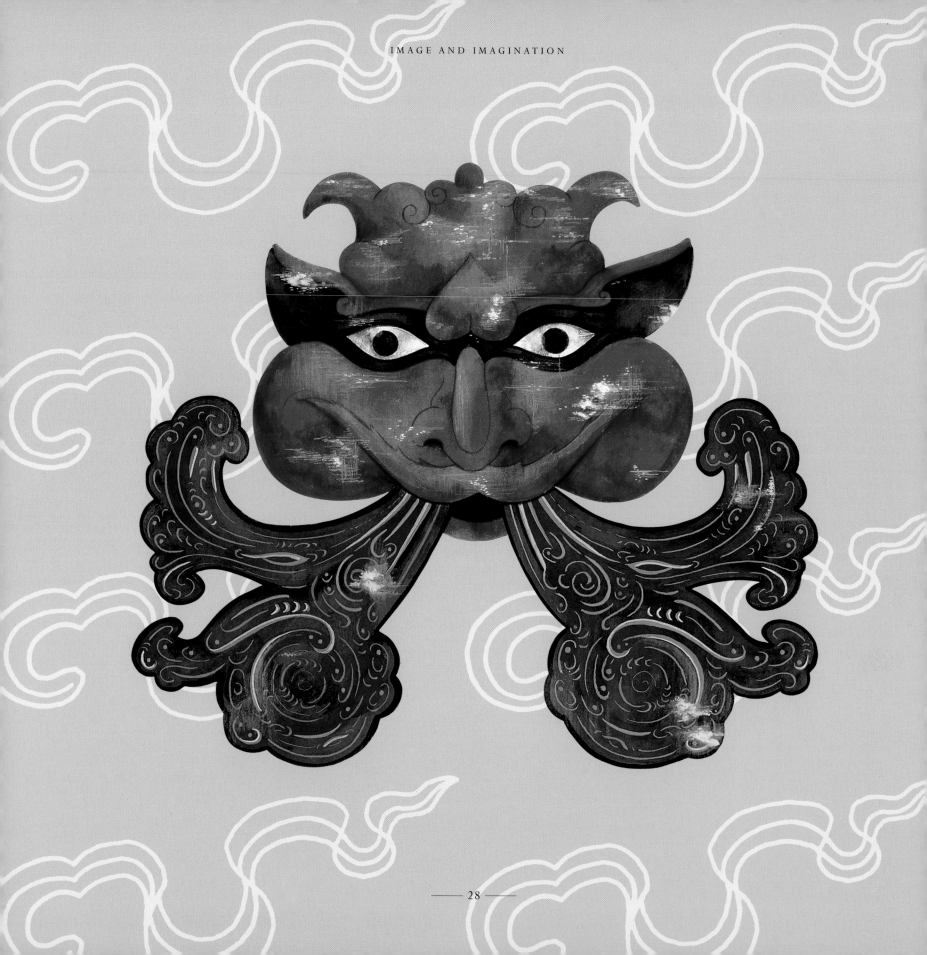

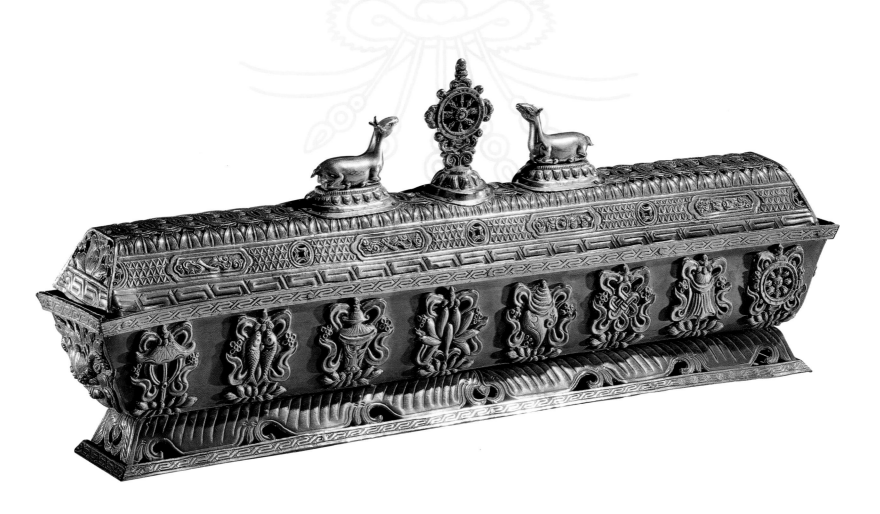

THE SPIRIT IN THE SMOKE

The use of incense is an important part of Tibetan ritual life and portable incense

burners are commonly found on Buddhist altars. Made of hammered metal in a

wide variety of shapes—from fierce heads with open mouths (left) to rectangular

boxes with pierced lids—incense burners are often decorated with the eight

auspicious emblems (see page 101). As well as the eight auspicious emblems, the

copper and silver example above also bears a "Wheel of *Dharma*" flanked by two

deer, symbols of the Buddha's first sermon in the Deer Park at Sarnath.

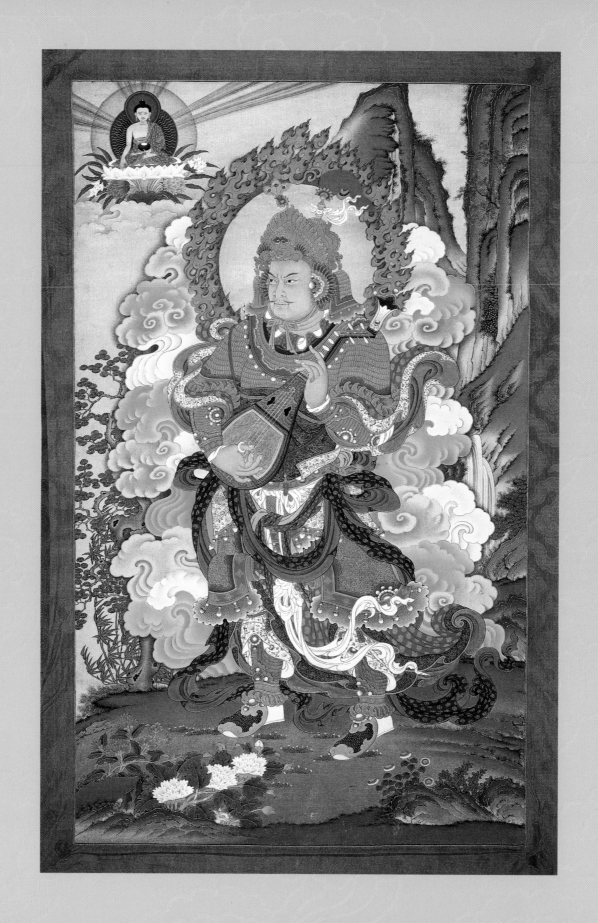

THE SACRED COSMOS

LEFT This 19th-century *thangka* painting shows Dhritarashtra, the guardian deity of the eastern quarter. He is regarded as the king of celestial musicians and for this reason holds a stringed instrument in his hands.

The Tibetan people perceive their country as a sacred cosmos, a holy landscape guarded by mighty gods and filled with centers of ritual and mystical power. Within this landscape, every natural feature, every building, and every deed is charged with religious significance. Mountains are often the seats of awe-inspiring deities, their caves places for meditation, and their winding trails emblematic of the path to enlightenment. By marking the landscape with cairns, inscriptions, rock paintings, banners, and votive offerings, Tibetans perpetually reinvent their world, reaffirming the lives of the ancient saints and sages whose heroic acts infused the universe with potent spiritual meaning.

BELOW Pilgrims are shown making their way around the Tashilhunpo monastery on the western edge of Shigatse. Tashilhunpo is the seat of the Panchen Lama, traditionally the holiest religious leader in Tibet after the Dalai Lama.

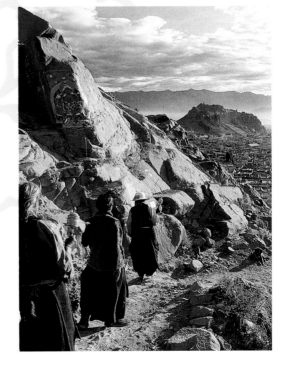

SPIRIT, SPACE, AND ENLIGHTENMENT

When Queen Bhrikuti came from Nepal in the seventh century CE to join the court of King Songtsen Gampo, she perceived the form of a great demoness in the landscape of Tibet. To subdue her, Bhrikuti decided that Buddhist temples should be built on the most prominent parts of the demoness's body. The heart—her most vulnerable point—was identified as a small lake in Lhasa. The lake was filled and the Jo Khang, Tibet's holiest temple, was erected on the site (see pages 22–23). Other "extremity-subduing" temples were built on what were believed to be the hips and shoulders of the demoness. The construction of these buildings put an indelible Buddhist stamp on the wider landscape of Tibet, effectively overpowering earlier ideas and beliefs. It was an ancient tactic, used even by the Buddha as a way of spreading his philosophical and social message.

The need to impose a new order on sacred space was faced again in the following century, when the monk-philosopher Shantarakshita wanted to establish Tibet's first Buddhist monastery at Samye near the Tsangpo River. Local demons are said to have interfered with every aspect of the construction. Unable to continue, Shantarakshita advised King Trisong Detsen to summon the great saint Padmasambhava from India. Padmasambhava came and drew a mystic diagram of the Five Transcendent Buddhas (see page 89) on the ground. After he had meditated on the diagram for seven days, the demons were powerless to stop the monastery from being constructed.

LEFT **Padmasambhava, regarded as a "second Buddha," was a great saint who is believed to have used his mystic powers to subdue demons opposed to the establishment of Buddhism in Tibet. In this 18th-century gilt bronze image, he holds a pronged thunderbolt (see page 86) and a vase containing the elixir of immortality.**

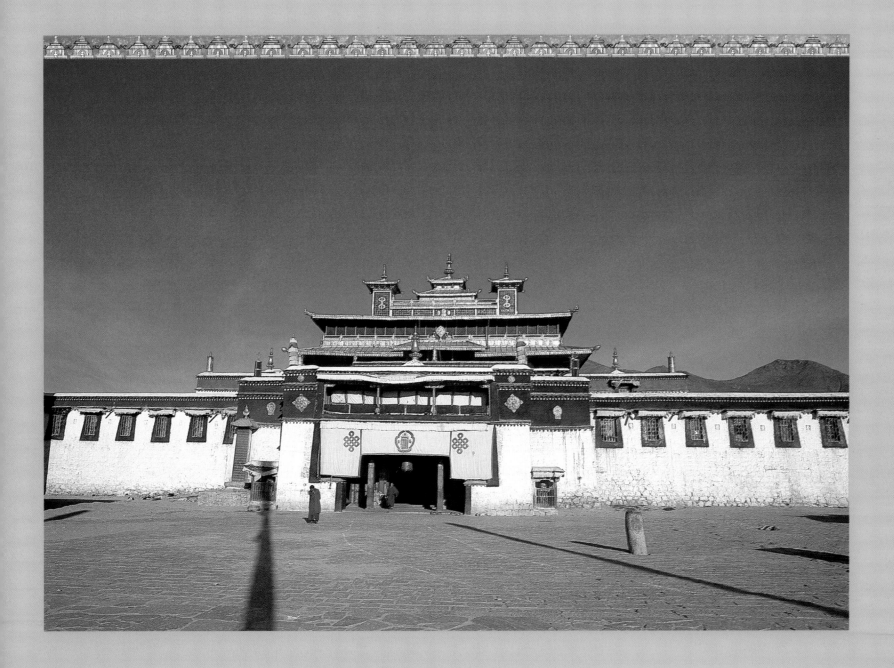

The Utse temple stands in the center of the 8th-century CE
monastic complex at Samye. The building has been much
modified over the centuries—the pinnacled roof of the
Utse, for example, has been entirely rebuilt since the 1980s.

UNFOLDING COSMIC SPACE

A *mandala* is a map of the Buddhist cosmos—the outer visible world, the forces that operate within it, and the deities, both great and small, that preside over it. Every element, force, and divinity in the universe corresponds to an aspect of the human personality and physiology, and an awareness of these links between the inner and outer worlds can bring special insight and mystical abilities to a Buddhist adept, or *siddha*. In Buddhism, however, the final goal is not simply knowledge and power, but a living and unbreakable awareness of the absolute unity of all existence. Those who have realized this truth enjoy enlightenment—a state of unshakable equanimity, supreme wisdom, and infinite compassion. *Mandala*s are aids in the pursuit of this enlightened state.

In Tibetan Buddhism, the development of an individual's potential is often visualized as the unfolding of a *mandala* in the form of a lotus. Each petal of the lotus is connected with certain deities, colors, and mystic sounds, or *mantra*s. The heart of the lotus represents the Absolute, the supreme being. Complicated esoteric rituals accompany the use of such *mandala*s and devotees undergo long periods of spiritual preparation so that the opening of a *mandala* is accompanied by a parallel "awakening" of the personality and soul. Inadequate preparation can make the whole ritual meaningless or, more catastrophically, unleash cosmic powers that would tear the individual apart.

Tibetan *mandala*s take many shapes and sizes, from small slips of paper with printed designs, to elaborate paintings, three-dimensional models, and even entire temples, such as the Kumbum at Gyantse (see page 36). Although paper *mandala*s are made in great numbers, their ephemeral nature has meant that few old specimens are preserved. Murals

LEFT (CLOSED) AND RIGHT (OPEN) **In the heart of this lotus *mandala* is a representation of Chakra Samvara, the esoteric manifestation of the Buddha. He is surrounded by female deities. The exterior of the lotus is engraved with the eight auspicious emblems (see pages 29 and 101).**

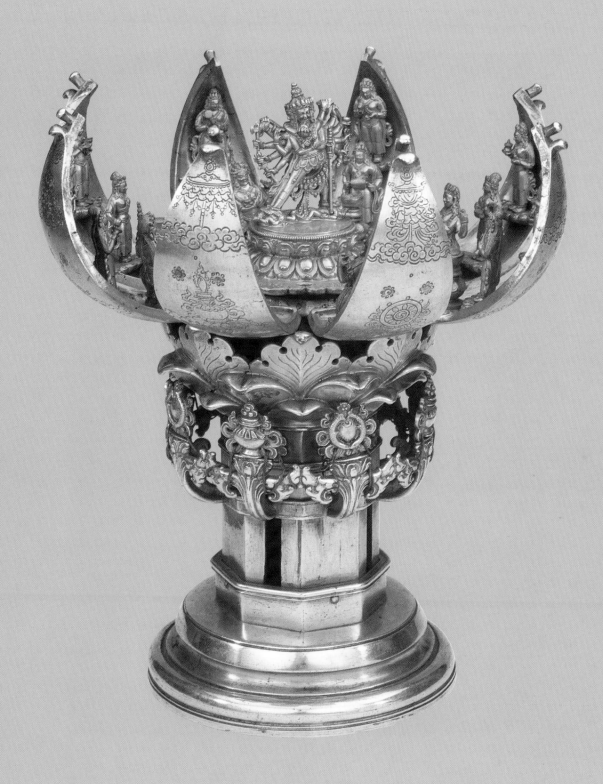

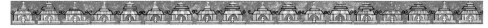

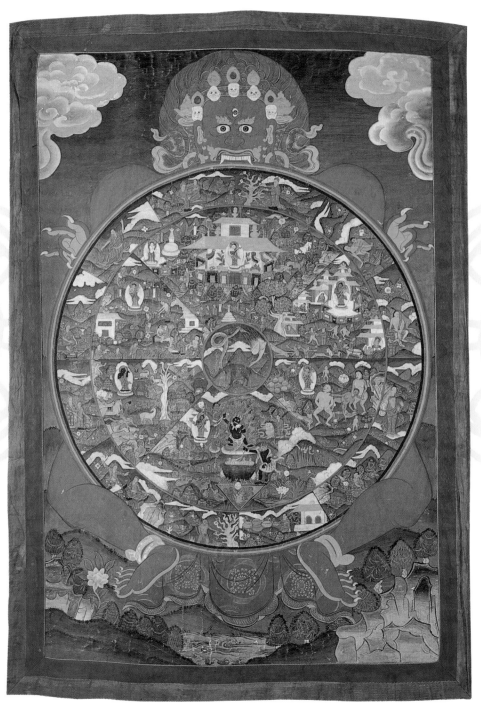

LEFT A *thangka* painting representing the "Wheel of Life" (*Bhavachakramudra*). It is divided into six parts, showing the various states of human life. The wheel is held by a hideous demon, symbolizing the human tendency to cling to material existence.

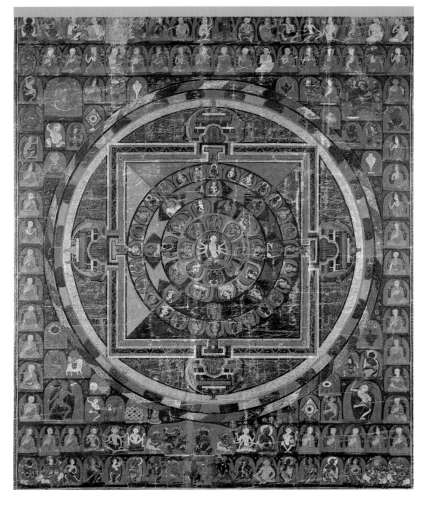

and painted scrolls are more common. Scrolls, or *thangkas*, are often edged with embroidered fabrics and have cloth covers to protect the painted surface.

RIGHT **This *mandala* shows Vasudhara, the divine consort of the cosmic Buddha, Vajra Sattva, seated in the middle of her emanations. Outside the sacred enclosure of the *mandala* are rows of seated holy Buddhist figures.**

Certain elements are common to most painted *mandala*s, which generally take the form of a circle within a square. A key feature is the deity (or deities) in the center of the image, whose divine presence the *mandala* is intended to invoke. The central figures are surrounded by emanations and related deities, typically placed on lotus petals. Encompassing these divine beings is a bold square enclosure, which is understood as a wall, with T-shaped gates halfway along each side. Outside the "gates" of the *mandala* there is a series of concentric circles decorated with lotus petals and other patterns, often waves and mountains. Beyond this lie rows of small figures, which typically represent protector-deities and saints.

An astonishing variety of *mandala*s resulted from the deft manipulation and elaboration of these basic ingredients. This is because the masters of the Tibetan tradition have had different visions of the path to enlightenment and have consequently developed their own repertoire of *mandala*s and meditation techniques.

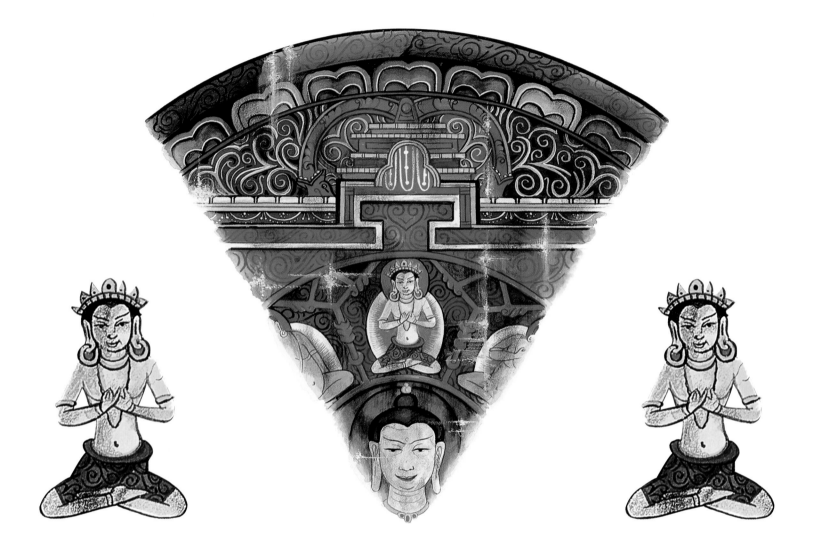

THE COSMIC CIRCLE

Most *mandala*s (see pages 34–37) consist of a single circle within a square. As they were often painted in sets—as in wall paintings in the temples at Alchi and elsewhere—it is not unusual for *mandala*s to be grouped together on one piece of cloth. The four-part *mandala* shown opposite depicts forms of Hevajra, the special protector deity of the Sakya-pa school of Tibetan Buddhism (see page 18). In the center are two seated teachers, or *lama*s, of the Sakya-pa.

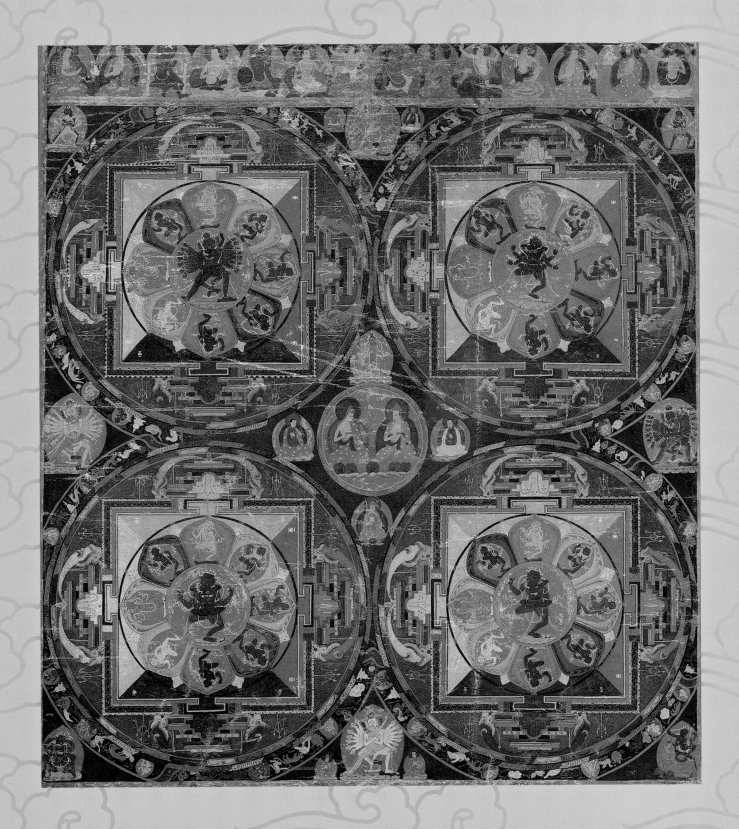

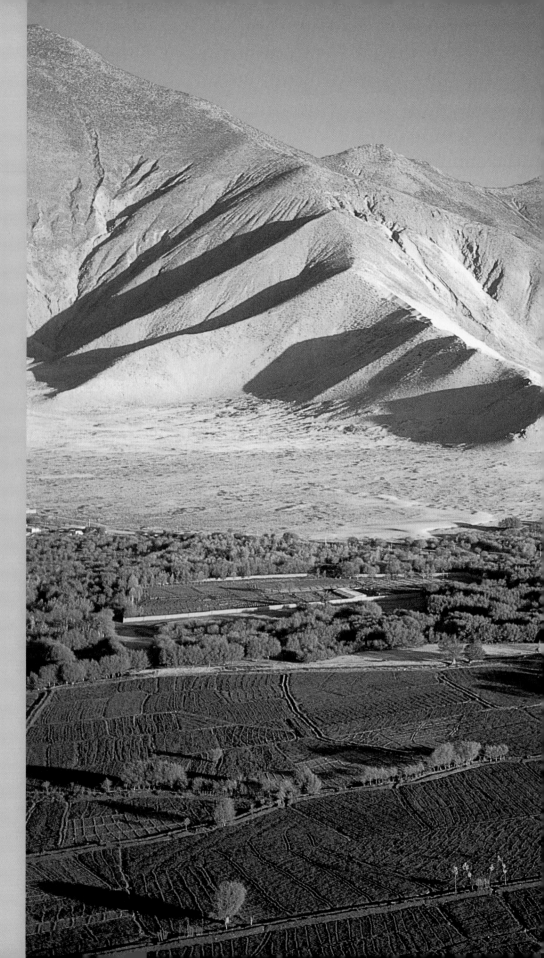

ARCHITECTURE OF ENLIGHTENMENT: SAMYE

Tibet's oldest monastery, Samye, was constructed
in the eighth century CE in a confidently eclectic
and international style under the auspices of
Shantarakshita and Padmasambhava. These Indian
holy men and their patron, the king of Tibet,
sought to create an entirely new place of religious
power and significance. By establishing the
institution of monasticism in Tibet, they aimed at
a complete reordering of Tibetan society, where-
by people would redirect their lives along the
Buddha's path to enlightenment and revolutionize
their ways of thinking, moving, and being.

Samye's architecture represents nothing less than
a fresh vision of the universe: the whole monastic
settlement constitutes, in effect, a gigantic Buddhist
cosmic diagram—a *mandala* (see pages 34–37). The
outer walls are circular in design and the buildings
within reflect the Buddhist cosmos. In the center,
a large multistoried temple—traditionally said to
combine Indian, Chinese, and Tibetan styles—
represents Sumeru, the towering mountain at the
heart of the Buddhist universe. Flanking it, and
representing the four continents, are four *chortens*,
or sanctuaries, in different colors and styles. The
entrances are protected by figures of lions and
statues of guardian beings, of which the most
celebrated is the deity Pehar, who originated
in central Asia.

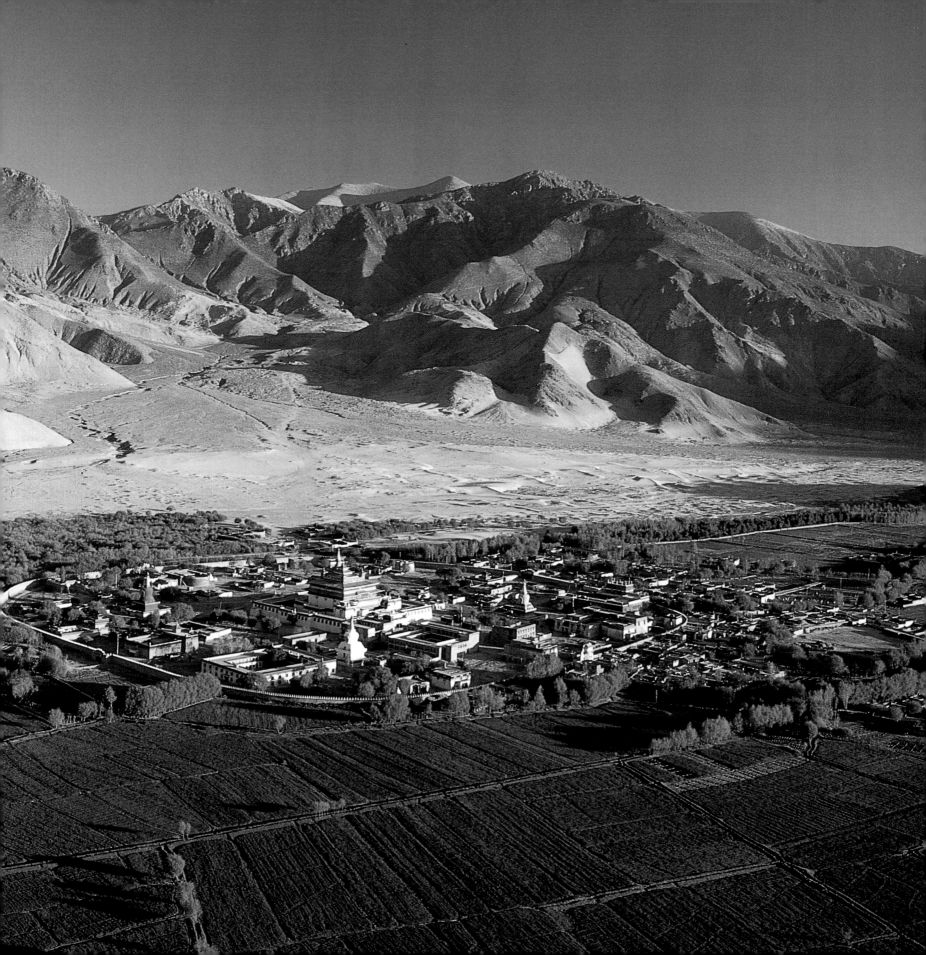

CITY OF SHRINES: GYANTSE

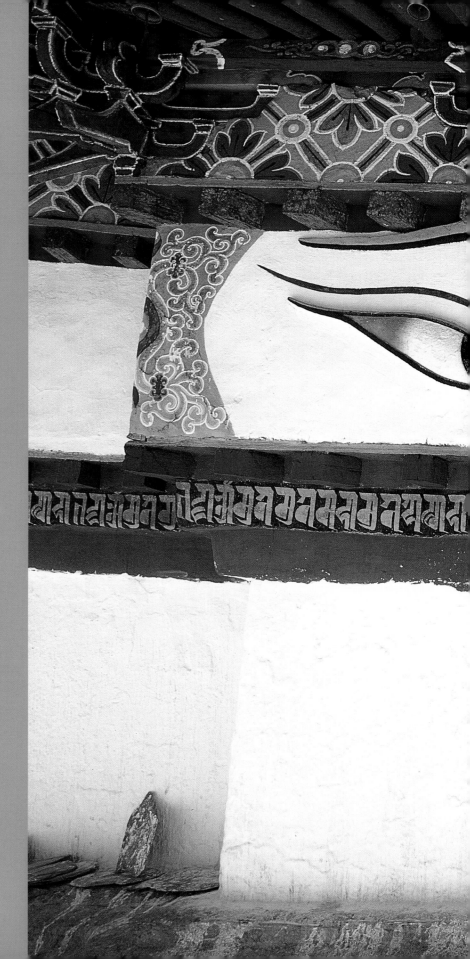

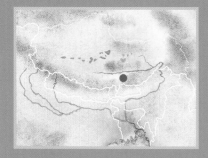

Once the third-largest town in Tibet after Lhasa and Shigatse, Gyantse was an important center for trade, mostly in wool, on the ancient road that led from Tibet to Sikkim, Bhutan, Nepal, and eastern India. Travelers and monks had passed this way for centuries, but Gyantse's heyday came only in the fifteenth century CE, when it was the capital of a small but prosperous Tibetan kingdom. It was this period that saw the construction at Gyantse of one of Tibet's most extraordinary sacred monuments, the magnificent three-dimensional *mandala*, known as the Kumbum.

The town grew up alongside a line of curving hills edged with walls and towers. Nestled next to the hillside is a self-contained monastic quarter that once housed a cluster of monasteries belonging chiefly to the Sakya-pa and Gelug-pa traditions (see pages 16–18).

The ever vigilant and watchful eyes of the Buddha look out from the summit of the Kumbum at Gyantse. The temple was built by craftsmen and artists from Tibet and Nepal in the 15th century.

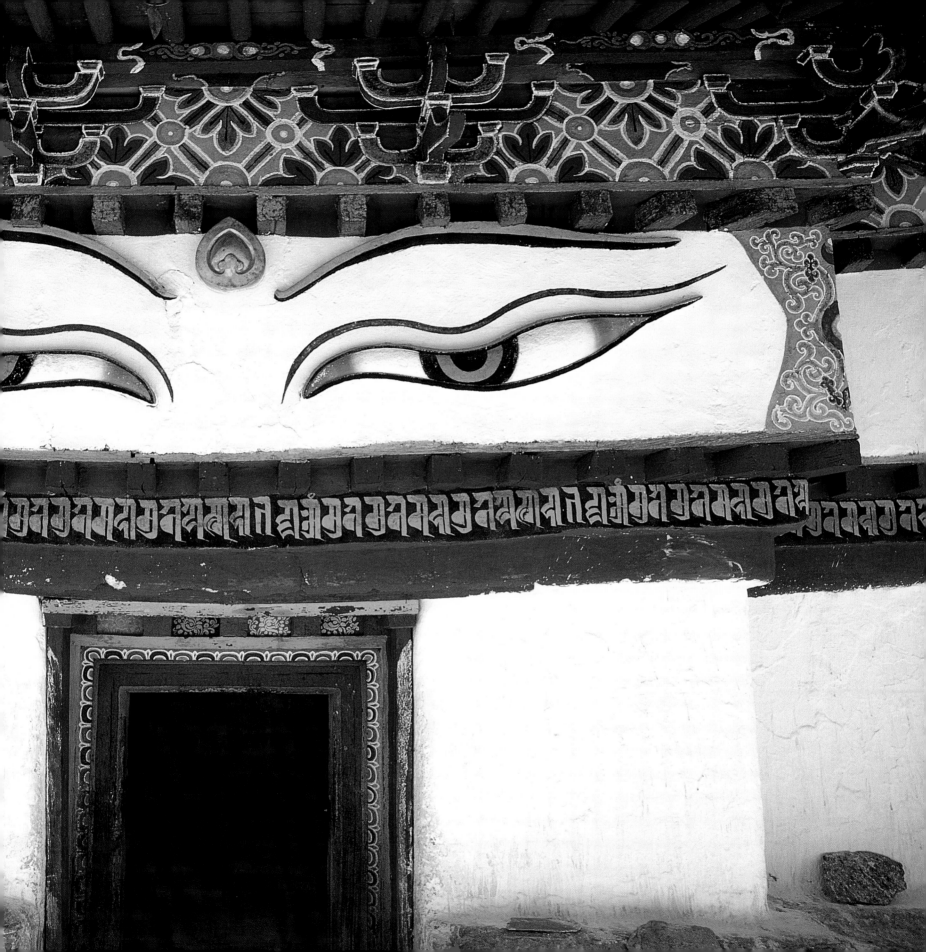

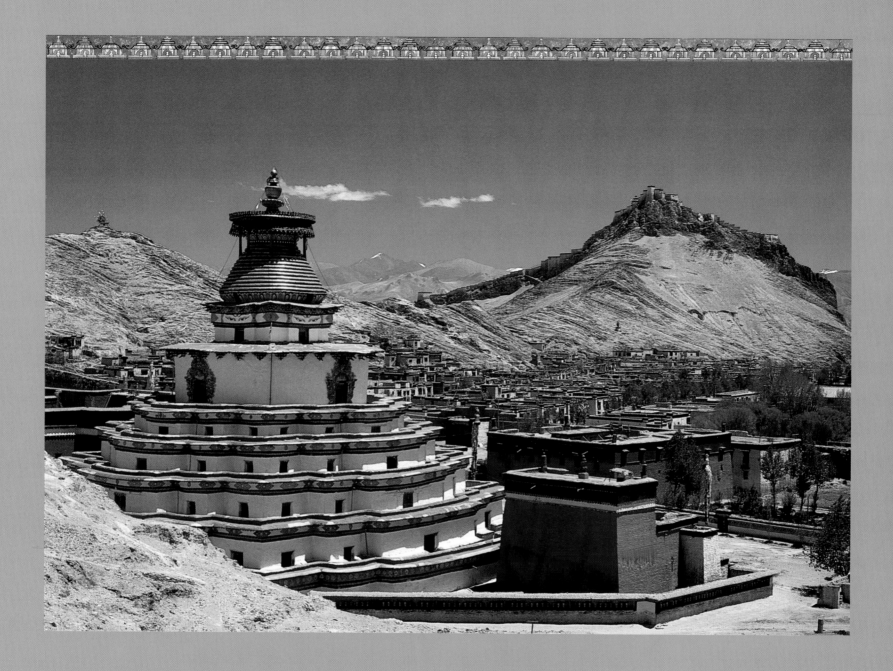

A view of Gyantse with the celebrated Kumbum in the foreground. In
the distance is the hilltop fortress of Gyantse, heavily damaged in 1904
by a British military expedition led by Francis Younghusband.

The Kumbum is the best-preserved and most elaborate temple of its type in all of Tibet. Consecrated in 1436CE, it was built during the reign of Prince Rabtan Kunzang Phags (1412–1442), the chief patron of the Gyantse complex. During this period, famous Tibetan painters and sculptors were attracted to Gyantse to participate in the construction projects there, apparently assisted by craftsmen brought from Nepal.

The Kumbum temple consists of a stepped pyramid surmounted by a circular drum and an elaborate conical spire. Inside there are more than seventy separate chapels, each filled with images and murals of Buddhist deities. A dark and narrow passage leads to the small shrine room at the top of the Kumbum, which contains an image of Vajra Dhara, the cosmic Buddha (see page 86), which the Gelug-pa tradition regards as supreme and absolute.

Through its architecture and its multitude of images, the Kumbum represents a total model of the Buddhist cosmos. From base to summit, all things find a proper and ordered place, and the devotee, by moving through the temple, participates in and reaffirms the Buddhist vision of time, space, and causation. This idea of capturing the universe in a microcosmic model is encountered in *mandala*s, which are most commonly based on the form of a circle within a square (see page 34). The degree to which the *mandala* concept could be elaborated is wonderfully illustrated by the Kumbum, where the central circle has become a tiered finial with an umbrella-like top and the square, a stepped pyramid.

LEFT **The doors of this wooden model of a temple, which resembles the Kumbum at Gyantse, contain many images, each of which is set behind a small window. Inside the model, additional figures and images are hidden. Necklaces have been used like garlands to decorate the roof.**

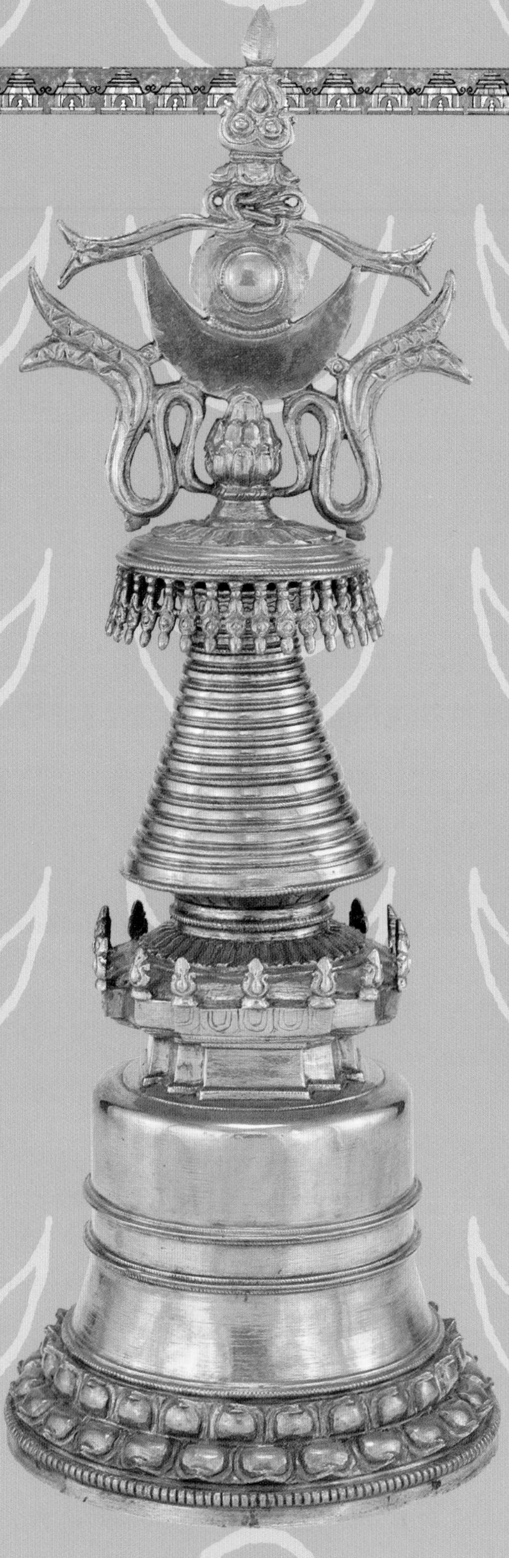

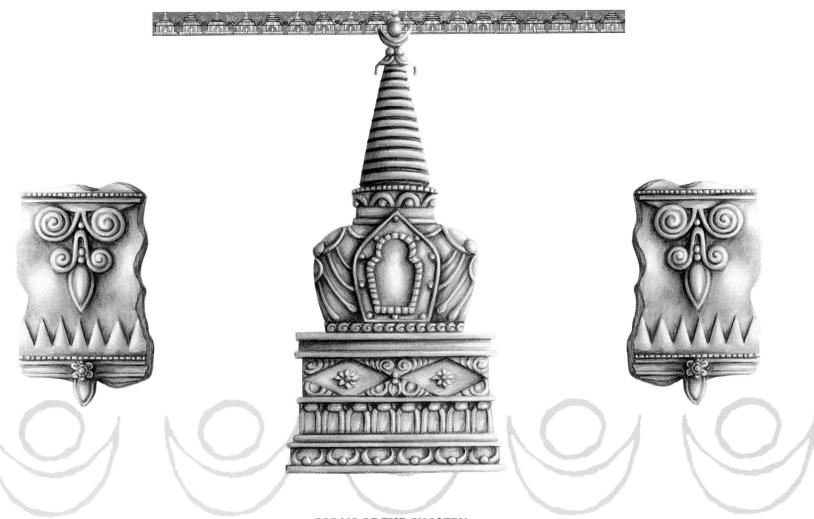

FORMS OF THE *CHORTEN*

In early India, mounds of earth, brick, and stone (*stupa*s) were used
to house holy Buddhist relics. This led to *stupa*s being seen as a
symbol of the Buddha's final liberation (*nirvana*). As their use spread
across Asia with Buddhism, *stupa*s retained their basic function as
relic containers. In Tibet, where they are called *chorten*s, the form
was employed not only for sacred burial monuments, but also for
metal reliquaries (opposite and above) that are kept on Buddhist
temple altars. Tibetan *chorten*s are surmounted by elaborate tiered
finials, often decorated with streamers and flags.

MOVING IN SACRED SPACE

Tibet's pilgrimage sites derive their significance from an ancient sense of place, a deep-rooted feeling that the mountains, lakes, and rivers are inherently places of purity and power. Nowhere is more sacred as a place of transcendence and personal renewal than Mount Kailas in the western Himalayas.

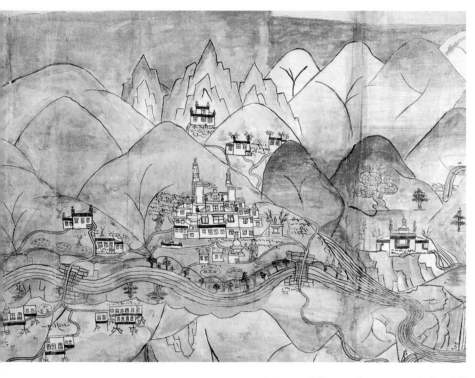

This detail of a long painting on cloth shows the sacred places and pilgrimage routes in the Tsari region in the eastern part of central Tibet.

From near the snow-capped peak of Kailas flow four of Asia's great rivers: the Indus, Sutlej, Tsangpo (Brahmaputra), and Karnali (the latter a tributary of the Ganga). Over the centuries, pilgrims have traced these rivers to their source and invested the region with overlapping and competing religious meanings.

Shiva, the great Hindu god, resides eternally on Kailas and for this reason, it is said, the Buddha chose Kailas as the place to appear as Chakra Samvara (see page 34), and instruct Shiva in the esoteric doctrines of Tantric Buddhism.

The Buddhists also engaged the followers of the Bon faith at Kailas, the mountain becoming a battleground between Naro Bon Chung and Milarepa, his Buddhist opponent. After many displays and counter-displays of mystic power, the two raced to the summit, Milarepa winning the contest by miraculously riding to the mountaintop on the rays of the rising sun. Although the Bon lost control of Kailas, out of compassion they were still allowed to circumambulate the mountain in a counterclockwise direction according to their ancient traditions.

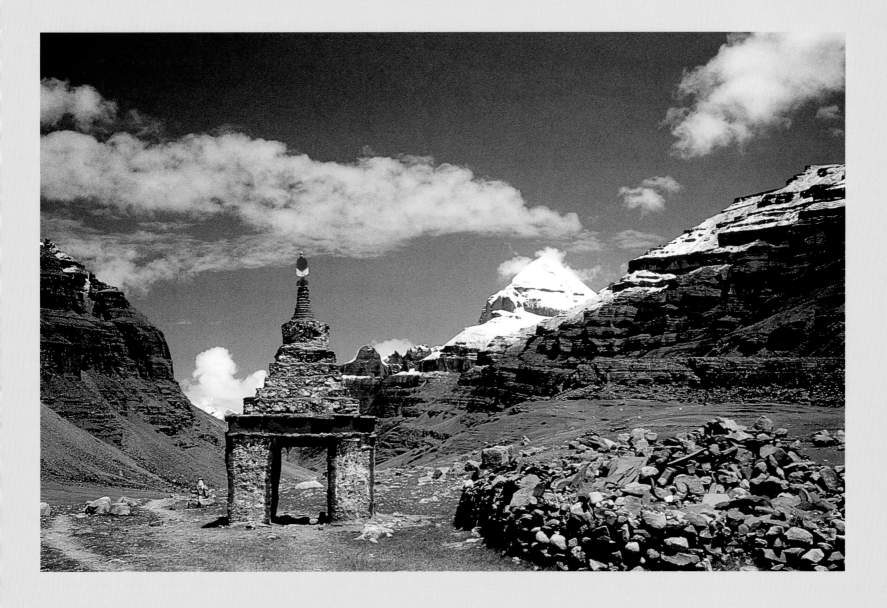

The difficulty and inaccessibility of Kailas is traditionally attributed to the power of the mountain itself, which allows only the pure and spiritually prepared to glimpse its mighty white pinnacle (above). Like all holy places, respects are paid at Kailas by circumambulation, the circuit around the mountain being an arduous high-altitude trek that can last several days. The route is marked by shrines, tablets inscribed with prayers, flagpoles, and caves associated with Milarepa and Padmasambhava.

SEEKING SOLITUDE
AND RETREAT

BELOW **Milarepa is usually shown with one hand raised—a gesture used to indicate that he is reciting one of his celebrated poems or hymns—as in this 18th- or 19th-century bronze figure of the saint.**

The Buddha had only five followers when he first began to spread his teachings, but from this humble beginning the Buddhist community grew into a large and powerful organization. An extensive code of regulations, the *Vinaya*, was soon needed to control all aspects of monastic life and from the Buddha's time to the present most monks have lived in highly organized monasteries. This pattern is especially predominant in Tibet, where monasteries are the main cultural and social institutions in the landscape.

Despite the importance of monasticism, Buddhism has never lost sight of the fact that the Buddha achieved *nirvana* as a solitary seeker and that all who strive for enlightenment must find it by, and within, themselves. Each of the great masters of Tibetan Buddhism have stayed for long periods in lonely places and in isolated caves, pursuing perfection and liberation.

Milarepa, Tibet's most beloved saint, lived a completely itinerant life. In his youth, he was vengeful by nature and practiced sorcery and black magic. However, filled with remorse about his evil ways, Milarepa turned to Marpa, a teacher in the south of Tibet who had studied for long periods in the great Buddhist monasteries of eastern India. After undergoing an exceptionally arduous apprenticeship, Milarepa was initiated into the secrets of Buddhist meditation and in particular into the mystical practices of Naropa, Marpa's Indian master. Naropa was a "Great Adept," or *Mahasiddha*—a title bestowed on eighty-four especially

RIGHT **Peaks and high mountain passes are frequently ornamented with flags and banners, offerings which are believed to distribute blessings across the landscape as they flutter in the wind.**

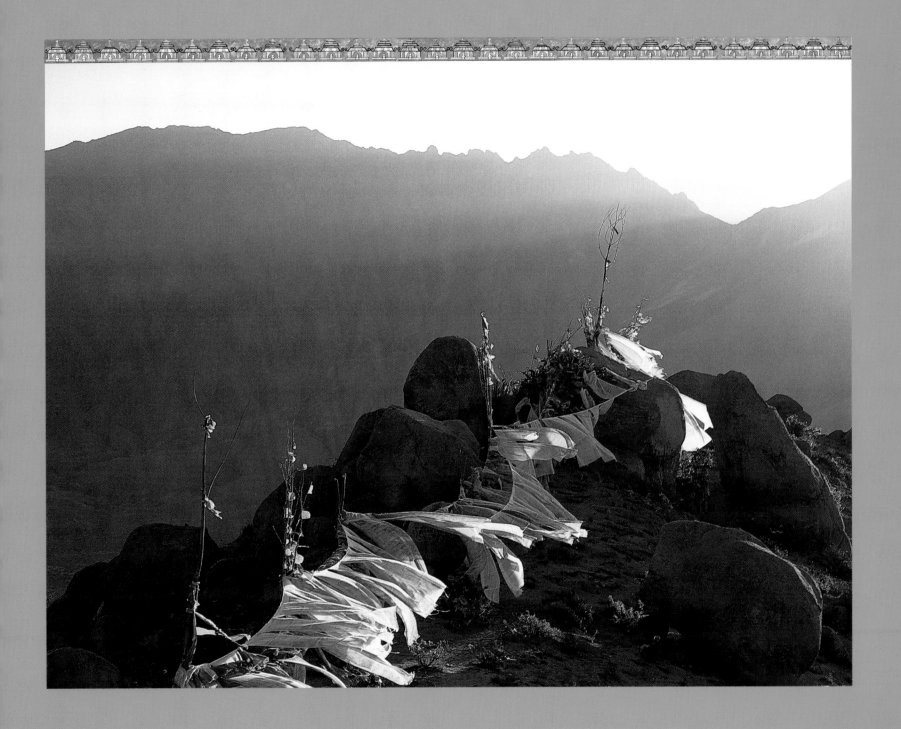

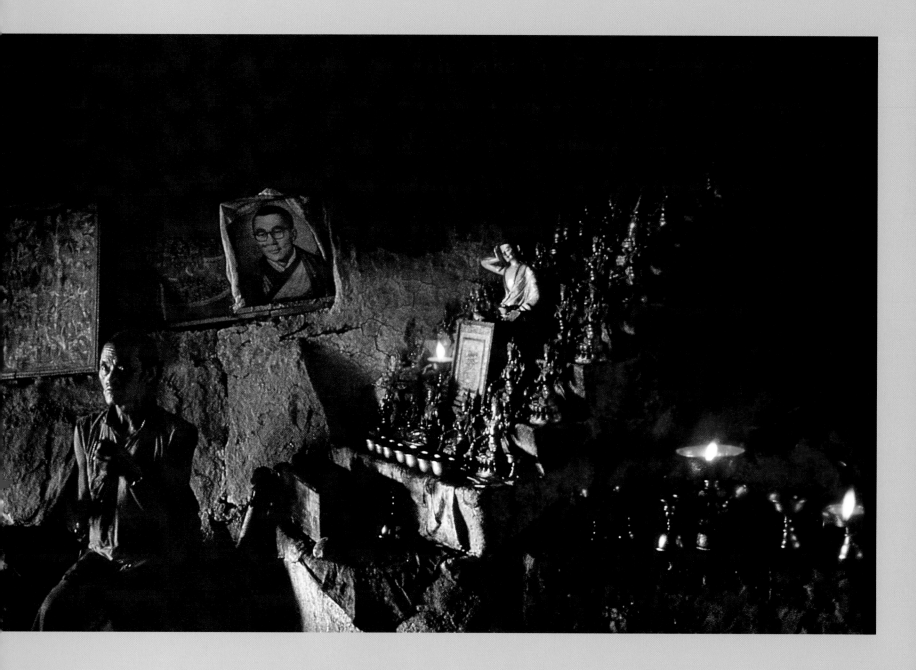

Milarepa spent years in isolated mountain caves, perfecting his powers and
seeking liberation. Tibetan caves, such as the one shown here, are widely dedicated
to Milarepa and often watched over by monks who, following the saint's example,
shun the comforts of ordinary life as part of their spiritual training.

holy saints known for their extrasensory insights and superhuman powers. The Great Adepts developed the teachings and texts used by the Kagyu-pa and related Tibetan schools (see page 16).

Milarepa's command of Naropa's teaching gave him astonishing physical strength and enabled him to withstand the bitterly cold Himalayan winters. He left southern Tibet and continued his spiritual quest in the solitude of the mountains. Wandering westward, he came to the Namkading cave near Nyalam, where he spent such long periods in meditation that there are impressions in the rock where he sat.

Like all renunciates before and since, Milarepa fled to lonely places in order to pursue the contemplative life. However, retreat from the world meant leaving the secure structure of civilized life and venturing into places that were the haunt of wild and malevolent forces. These forces were both the evils within the human heart and the ancient deities and foes of Buddhism. Milarepa was victorious over his own evil past and vanquished the Bon deities at Mount Kailas (see page 48). Consequently, he is revered by Tibetans—together with Padmasambhava and the Buddha himself—as one of the great trio of enlightened "Conquerors," who used their inner spiritual power to transform hostile gods into protectors of the Buddhist faith.

Milarepa never established a monastery or belonged to one of the religious orders. However, statues of him are found throughout the country, while his marvelous poems and songs are quoted everywhere.

RIGHT **Nagpopa was a Great Adept (*Mahasiddha*), who came to Tibet from India in the 11th century. There are many legends about him, including the story that he lived for several hundred years and was none other than the Indian monk Bodhidharma, whose teaching influenced the Chan and Zen schools of Buddhism in China and Japan.**

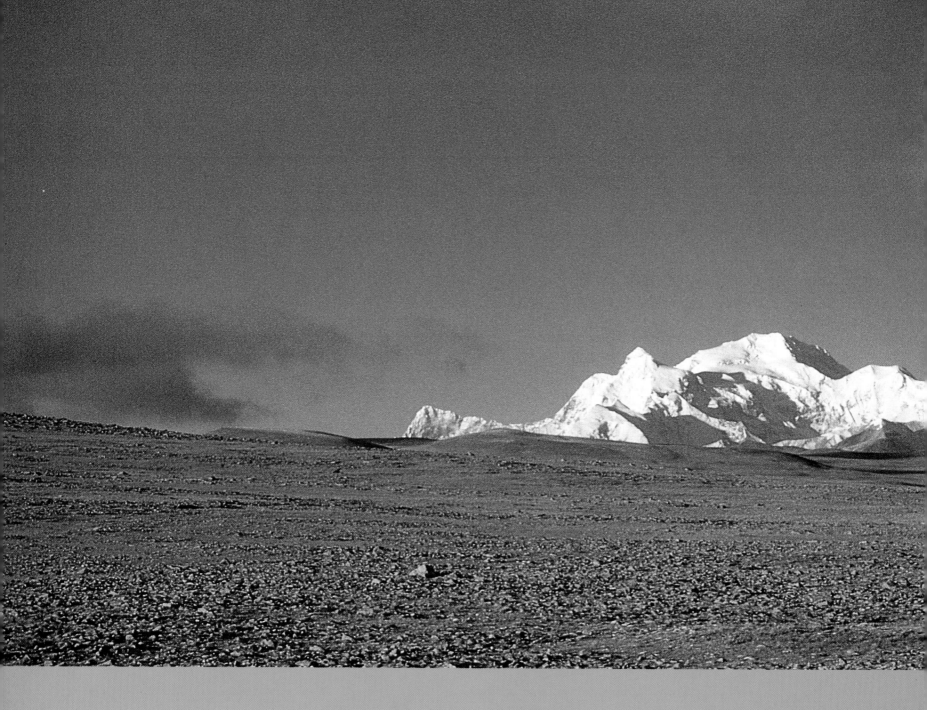

MALEVOLENT REALMS

Tibet, "the Roof of the World," is the highest country on earth and even its capital, Lhasa, one of the lowest points, is some 3,590 meters (11,800 feet) above sea level. The severity—and, in Tibetan belief, potential malevolence—of much of the Tibetan environment is nowhere more extreme than on the great northern plateau, the Jang Tang, shown here. With an average elevation of 4,500 meters (14,800 feet), it is a vast high-altitude wilderness.

Dotted with brackish lakes, the Jang Tang is known for its severe weather system, which includes biting winds—so ferocious, in fact,

that travelers who pass through the region have been known to arrive at their destinations suffering from sunburn on one side of their faces and frostbite on the other. Only a few wandering herdsmen inhabit this desolate place.

Other parts of the land are less hostile. In spite of their altitude, Tibet's southern valleys are not inhospitable, and the fertile areas alongside the rivers produce barley, oats, beans, and other basic staples. However, on the mountain slopes above, only seasonal grazing is possible, while the high peaks are completely barren and usually covered in snow year-round.

DISEASE, DANGER, AND DEMONS

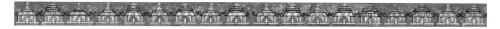

From the traditional Tibetan point of view, the world is a place pulsating with forces that directly influence all aspects of life. Rocks, rivers, trees, and the soil are all inhabited by spirits, which need propitiation before a tree is cut, the ground plowed, or the natural order of things otherwise disturbed by human action. The heavens, too, are filled with gods, some of them demonic huntsmen who, if angered, can cause sickness and death.

As in India, serpent-kings (*naga-raja*s) are connected with fertility, crops, and water. The association with water, and the potential malevolence of the serpents, is illustrated by the story of the snakes in the lake where Lhasa's Jo Khang temple now stands (see pages 22–24): when the lake was filled in, the snakes were taken and detained in a cave on the sacred mountain of Chakpori at Lhasa. Serpent-kings are the guardians of treasure, generally understood in Buddhist contexts to be relics, the elixir of immortality, and the *chinta-mani* ("radiant thought-gem," see pages 78–81). The great enemy of serpents is the eagle-headed Garuda, who is always depicted with a snake in his beak. He restores the *chinta-mani* to its rightful place in the lotus of Avalokiteshvara; relics to proper worship in *stupa*s; and the pot of elixir to Amitayus, the Buddha of Infinite Life.

With its ancient emphasis on detachment and renunciation, the high traditions of Buddhism offered few remedies for people who had to deal with a world fraught with real dangers. As a consequence, almost all Buddhist societies, including Tibet, have traditionally possessed various classes of shamans and healers.

Evil influences might be subdued by a type of ritual dagger known as a *phur-bu*, which has also found a place in Buddhist rites. When controlled by a shaman, a *phur-bu* is thought to be able to pin down evil spirits, fly through the air, destroy

LEFT **Ritual daggers (*phur-bu*s) for combating evil forces are unique to Tibetan Buddhism. This 19th-century bronze *phur-bu* includes the potent image of a god and goddess in union (see page 102).**

RIGHT **The eagle-like Garuda is one of the great protectors against malevolent forces, and known in ancient myths as a destroyer of snakes and a guardian of the elixir of immortality. In Tibet, some of the "Red Hat" schools have taken Garuda as their emblem. This 19th-century representation of Garuda is made from gilded wood.**

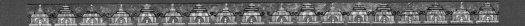

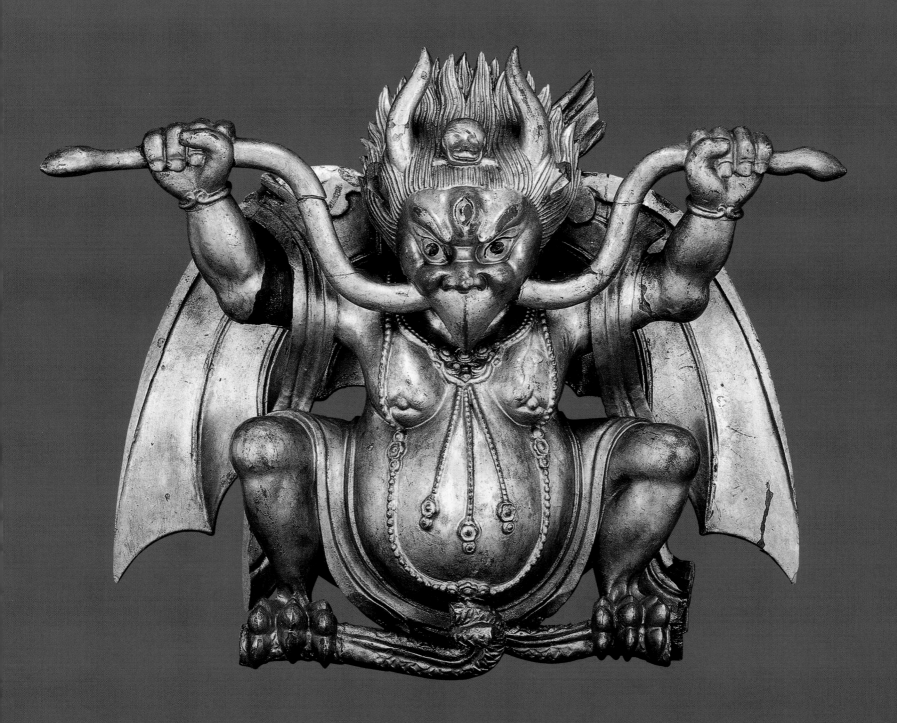

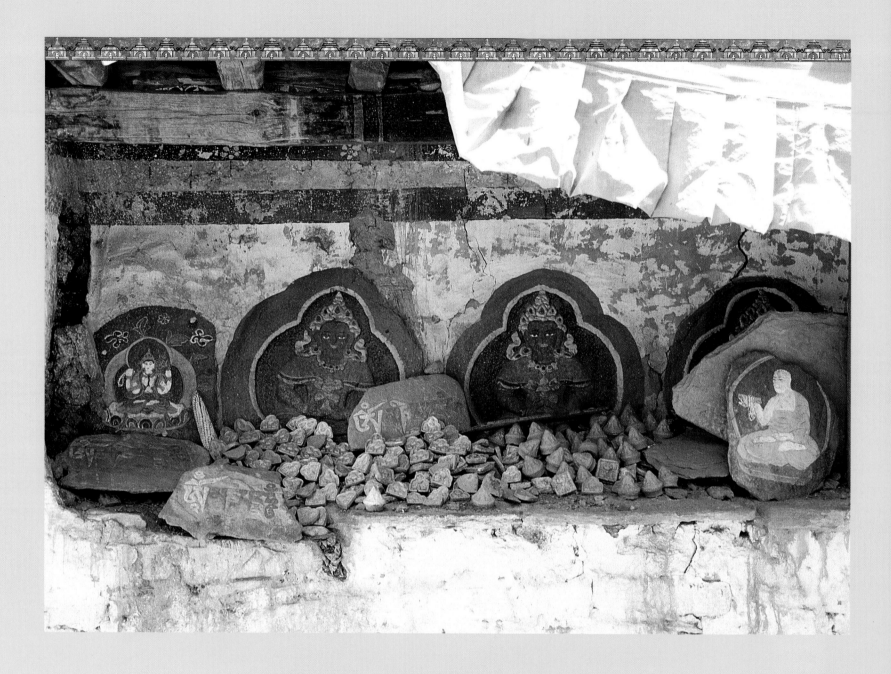

Small clay tablets and *chorten*s, pressed from molds, are often left
at informal shrines by Tibetan pilgrims. Here, numerous talismanic
votive offerings, or *tsha-tsha*, have been deposited at Ganden,
a monastic site approximately 25 miles (40km) east of Lhasa.

enemies, and control the weather. Scapegoats and scapegoat ceremonies were also once widespread in Tibet. Individuals, usually of low social rank, were called upon to take on the evils of the community and were chased away in elaborate parades, in which monks wore ferocious masks and colorful costumes. Less dramatic were small wooden "ransom sticks," used to remove or avert the afflictions caused by spirit possession. Most illness was explained as the work of evil spirits which needed to be exorcised if health was to be restored.

Tibetans take a pragmatic view of life and acknowledge that just as illness, adversity, and peril cannot be completely eliminated from human affairs, so demonic and malevolent deities can never be finally destroyed. At best, they can be contained and redirected, held in place by prayers, meritorious deeds, and the faithful maintenance of appropriate ritual.

One especially common way of reinforcing and maintaining sanctity, both of holy places and of the devotee, is through talismans and votive offerings. Found throughout the Buddhist world and termed *tsha-tsha* in Tibet, talismans are left in great numbers at sacred places and at pilgrimage spots. They are made of clay and stamped with sacred images, *chorten*s, and holy texts. Clay *tsha-tsha*s may contain sanctifying substances, such as the ashes of an especially holy monk. These are much prized and worn as protective amulets.

Perhaps the most poignant indication of how the Tibetan tradition has recognized the necessary coexistence of good and evil is the *gon-khang*, a separate chamber found in many Buddhist temples. Such rooms are reserved for ancient fierce and horrible gods, who are now considered to be the custodians and protectors of the very sacred places that once belonged to them, but from which they were expelled after the arrival of Buddhism.

This 12th-century bronze seal (above), with an accompanying modern clay impression (left), depicts the seated figure of a Bodhisattva. Such seals are used to mass-produce the small tablets (*tsha-tsha*) used as votive offerings.

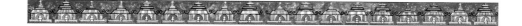

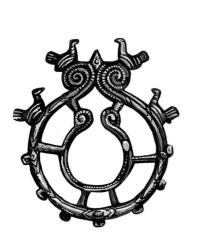

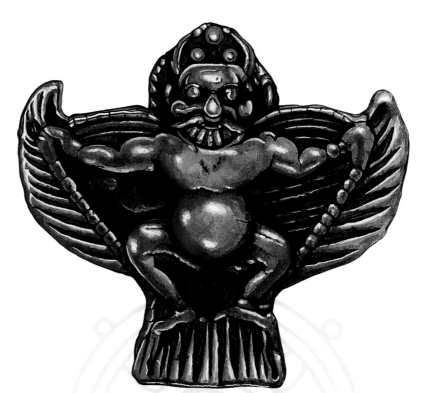

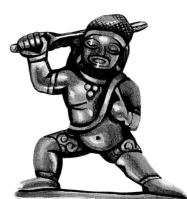

CHARMS AND AMULETS

Tibetan charms and amulets are made in the form of various
deities and auspicious emblems, as above. Some—traditionally,
small, painted clay tablets—are kept in amulet boxes believed
to protect the wearer from evil influences. As amulet boxes are
portable shrines, they are often placed on domestic altars. The
wooden box shown opposite contains a clay tablet depicting
Avalokiteshvara seated on a lion.

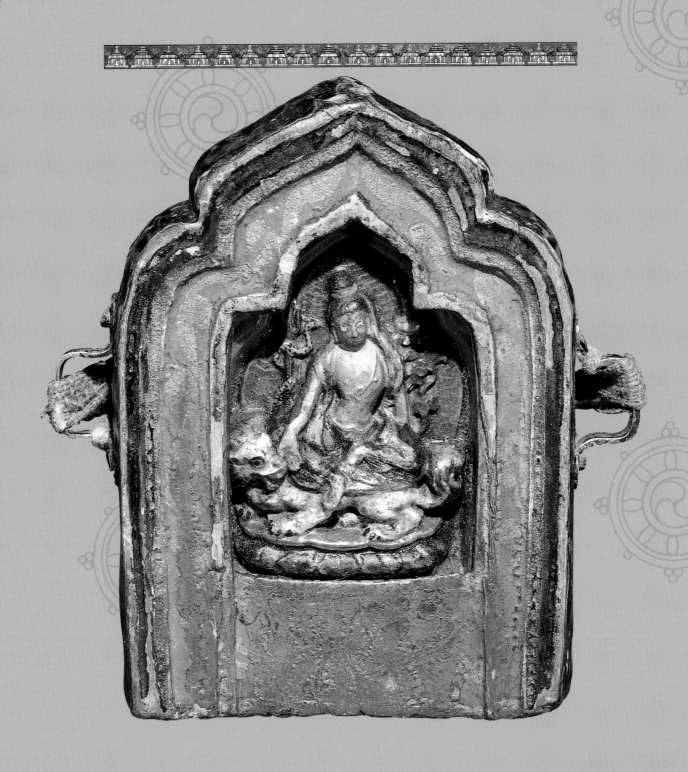

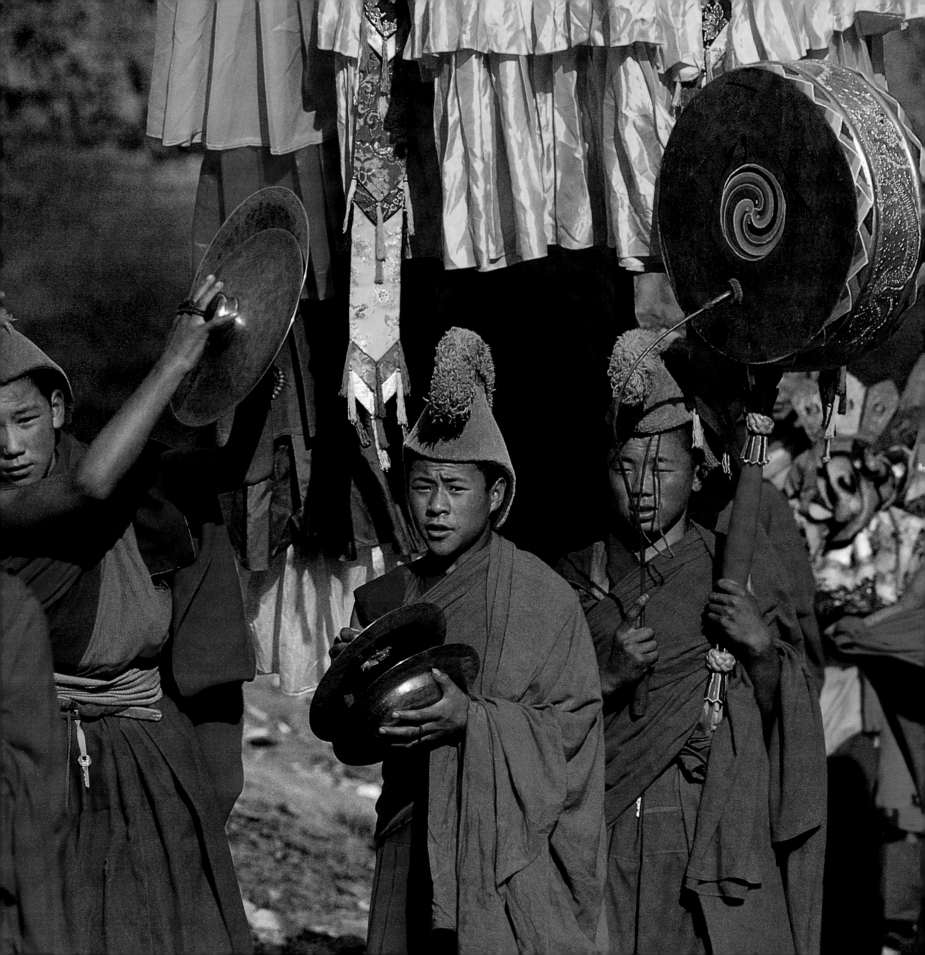

INVOKING THE DIVINE

The sacred world of Tibet is filled with the chanting of Buddhist texts, the recitation of *mantras*, the ringing of bells and cymbals, the blowing of trumpets, and the beating of drums. All are essential aspects of Buddhist life and ritual. The rich variety of books and musical instruments—and the care with which they are made, decorated, and consecrated—are testimony to the key role of sacred words and sounds in the Tibetan tradition. The potency of sound goes back to the the story of how Sariputra, one of the Buddha's chief disciples, gained enlightenment by simply hearing the words of the Buddhist creed: "The Buddha has explained the cause of all created things and how to contain that cause as well."

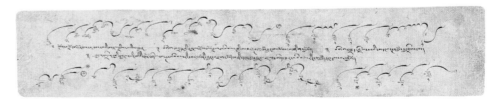

MUSIC AND RITUAL

Although silent meditation is a prominent aspect of Buddhism, large processions and noisy rituals, accompanied by all manner of music and dance, have also been integral to Buddhist religious life since at least the first century BCE. At Sanchi, in central India, early relief carvings at the great *stupa* depict religious processions with drummers, dancers, and pairs of trumpet blowers. This liturgical tradition was taken to Tibet when Buddhism was first introduced there in the seventh century CE, and almost all Tibetan ceremonies involve chanting and the use of musical instruments. Most ceremonies are monastic services in which only monks participate, but there are also public spectacles involving music and dance, notably, in former times, the scapegoat ritual (see page 56) and the annual mystery play (*lha-'cham*). The play, performed at the year's end by monks in front of their monasteries, involved groups of masked dancers and centered on a human effigy, which was attacked and destroyed so that the New Year could start freshly purged of evil influence.

The most distinctive Tibetan instruments are those made from human bone, which is used as a reminder of the transitory nature of human existence. Trumpets fashioned from thighbones—which are fitted with mouthpieces and decorative metalwork inlaid with semiprecious stones—are traditionally thought to subdue demons and are frequently used in exorcism. They are featured in paintings of fierce deities (see page 122) and are played when these gods are worshiped. The same is true of Tibetan drums made from the tops of human skulls, which are based on the damaru, an

RIGHT Long trumpets are sounded from the rooftop of the Tibetan monastery of Nechung (near Dharamsala in India) to mark the beginning of a Buddhist ceremony. Because of their great size, such trumpets are made in sections so that they can be collapsed like telescopes when they are not in use.

RIGHT This drum is made from the tops of two skulls—the use of human bone serves as a constant reminder of the ephemeral nature of human life. Attached to the drum are clappers on strings, which strike the instrument when it is rotated using the leather thong.

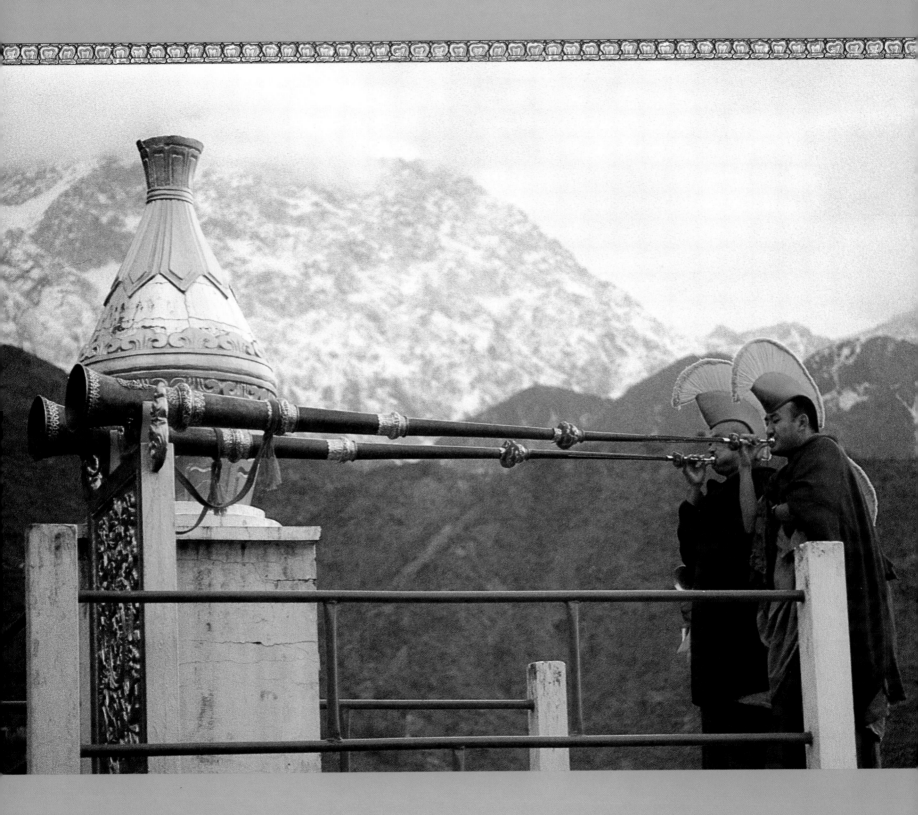

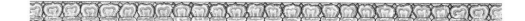

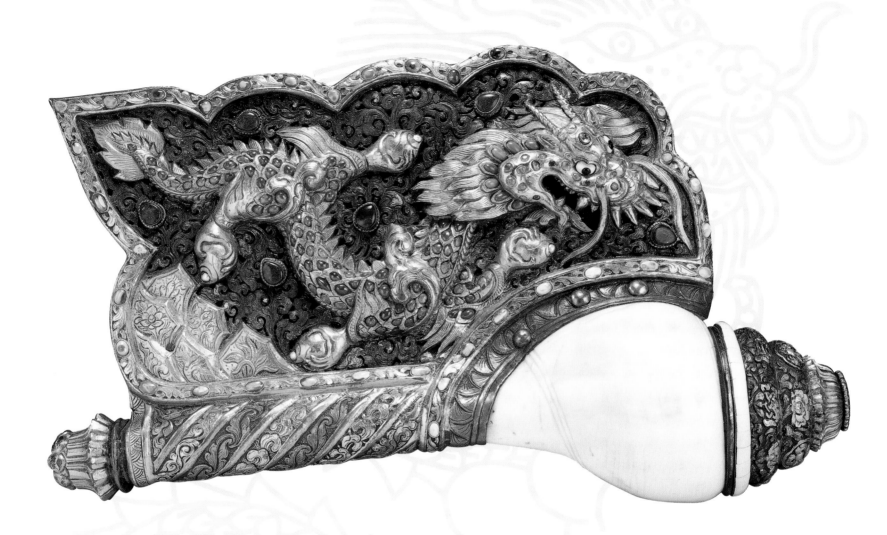

This conch-shell trumpet has a large metal flange decorated with a
dragon inlaid with precious stones. Dragons and other Chinese motifs
became increasingly common in Tibetan art during the 19th century.

ancient Indian double-ended drum shaped like an hourglass. In addition to their use in exorcism, these skull drums are played during recitations.

Conch-shell trumpets are unique to India and Tibet. Brought to the Himalayas from the distant Indian coasts, conchs are the instrument par excellence for heralding the gods, and they were once thought to release frighteningly destructive forces in time of battle. In Buddhist Tibet, conchs are employed for the more peaceful purpose of summoning monks to prayer, and in some areas they are also used to avert damage to crops from hailstorms. They are fitted with metal mouthpieces and tubes in order to deepen the sound they produce. Large decorative flanges set with colored stones are also added, as are fabric pendants.

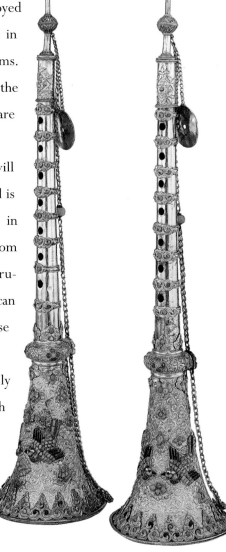

RIGHT **These silver shawms, which date from the 19th century, are heavily inset with turquoise, lapis lazuli, shell, and rubies. Like all Tibetan wind instruments, shawms are used in pairs so that the sound is not interrupted when one player pauses for breath.**

All Tibetan wind instruments are played in pairs: two musicians will play simultaneously, taking turns to breathe so that a continuous sound is produced. Large trumpets, some up to 5 meters (almost 16 feet) in length, produce a deep, haunting drone and are often sounded from rooftops to mark the beginning of ceremonies. Shawms (oboe-like instruments) have finger holes and are the only wind instruments that can produce a melody. They are used in almost all ceremonies, except those connected with exorcism.

Cymbals also enjoy wide usage. Large cymbals, which are generally stored in boxes of lacquered canvas, are used in the worship of both fierce and peaceful deities and to mark the beginning and end of liturgies. Small cymbals, no bigger than the palm of the hand and usually kept in little bags of Chinese silk, are used in private prayers; they make a wonderfully hypnotic sound that draws the mind into a state of calmness and tranquility.

SACRED SOUND

For more than three thousand years the civilizations of south Asia have placed great emphasis on the power of speech. Properly spoken and chanted words are not simple descriptions of the objective world, but holy sounds that are endowed with the very essence of the reality to which they refer. Sound has creative power, an actual capacity to influence objects and generate effects.

Such powerful, transforming words and phrases are called *mantras*, a technical term that literally means "instruments of thought." There are a great variety of *mantras* in Tibetan Buddhism. Some are an apparently random assortment of sounds and words with no logical meaning. But every *mantra* is intended for a specific purpose in worship or meditation and is designed to have specific effects on the individual and the immediate environment.

The knowledge of *mantras* is usually closely guarded and handed down from teacher to disciple without the details ever being committed to paper. However, some *mantras* are used by all Tibetan Buddhists as blessings and charms and are thought to be effective in all circumstances. The most popular of these is *Om mani padme hum* ("*Om* the Jewel of the Lotus *hum*"), the six-syllable prayer of Avalokiteshvara, the great Bodhisattva who is the patron deity of Tibet (see pages 94–95). This *mantra*—in which the first and last syllables have no specific meaning—is found everywhere in Tibet, whether printed on scrolls inside prayer wheels, carved on architectural panels, inscribed on boulders, or cut into the piles of stone that line well-trodden mountain passes. The *mantra* is counted on beads and forever brought to mind in moments of adversity, the invocation appealing again and again to the noble beneficence and compassion of Avalokiteshvara.

LEFT The *mantra* of Avalokiteshvara, the "Lord of Compassion," is the most popular in Tibet. This 19th-century standing figure of the great Bodhisattva in his eleven-headed form (see also page 97) is carved from wood and gilded. Delicately rendered dragons embellish the lower part of the drapery.

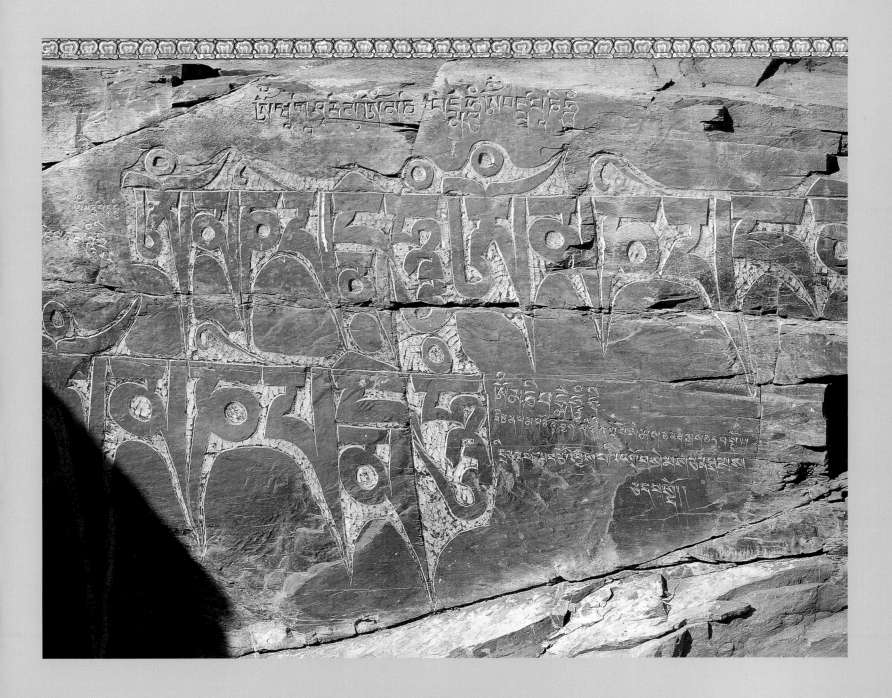

Om mani padme hum—the *mantra* of Avalokiteshvara—is
inscribed on this cliff-face at Lhasa. The talismanic inscription
is repeated on rocks and stone tablets throughout Tibet.

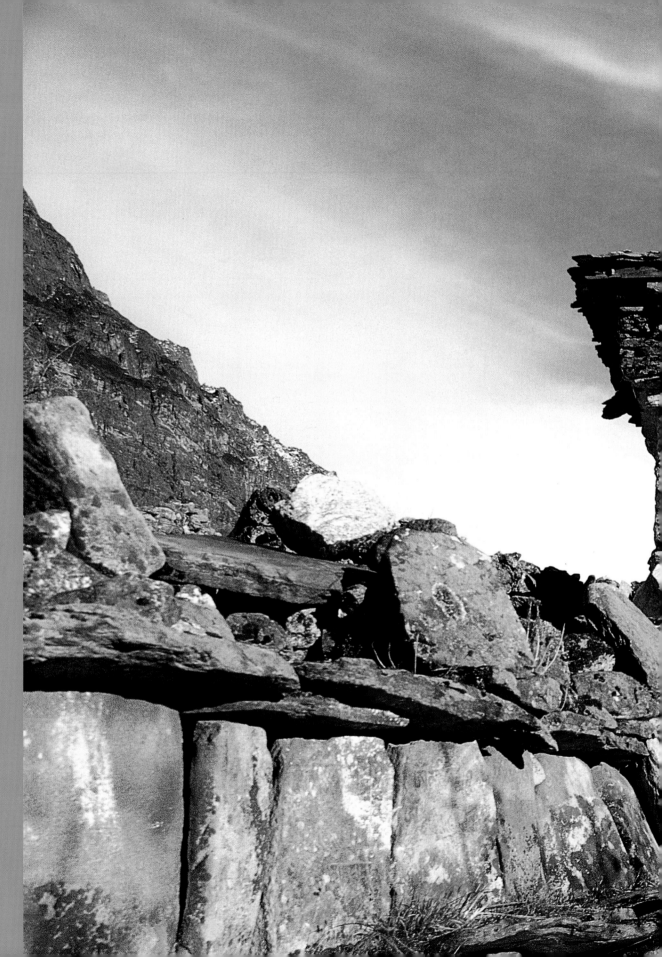

THE PATH OF THE MANI

On the ancient high-road from Kathmandu, the spectacular mountain pass of Langtan marks the border between the lush valleys of Nepal and the dry highlands of the Tibetan plateau. The pass is lined by cairns and carefully piled stones and slabs—some carved with *mandala* diagrams (see pages 36–37) and inscriptions, most commonly *Om mani padme hum* (see page 68). The conspicuous presence of this *mantra* at Langtan thus guards the entrance to Tibet with holy invocations of Avalokiteshvara, the patron deity and protector of the Tibetan people.

It was through this and similar passes that all the trade goods between Tibet, Nepal, and India were transported. Mules, yaks, and donkeys were the most common beasts of burden, carrying furs, hides, yak tails, borax, salt, musk, and medicinal herbs.

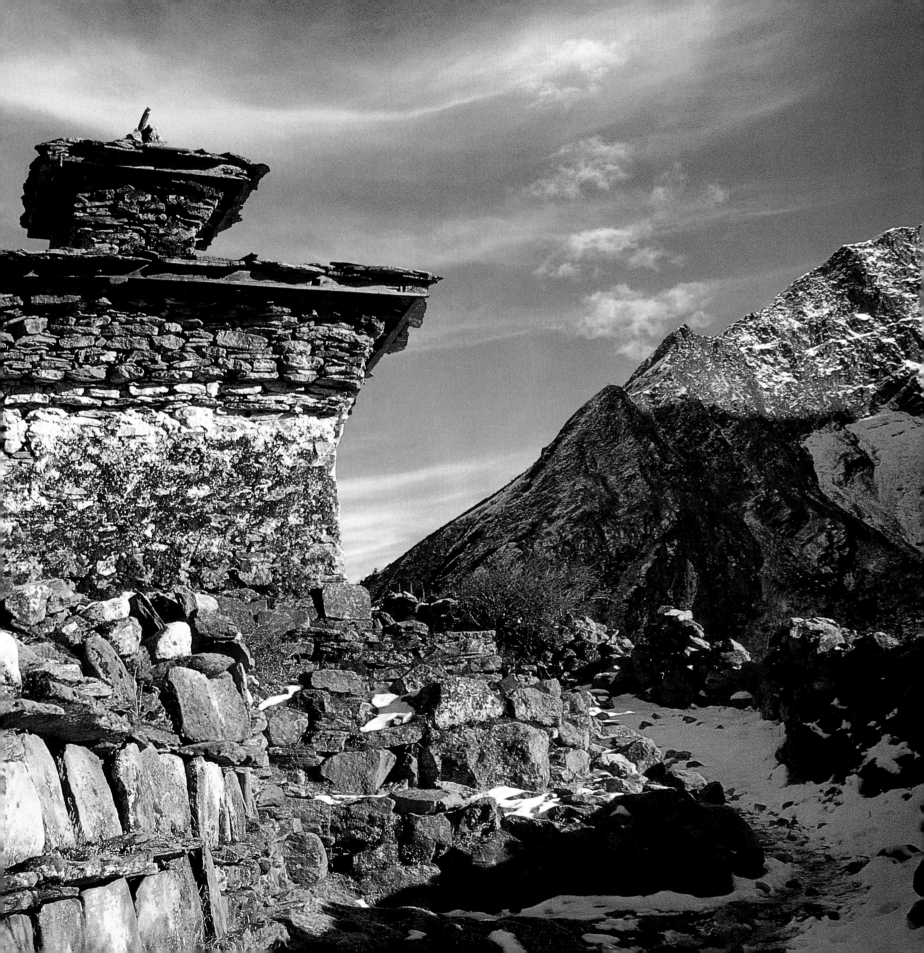

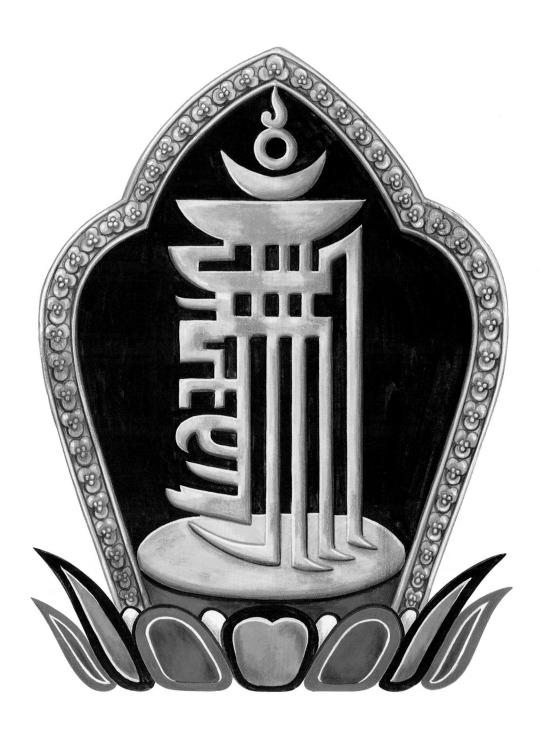

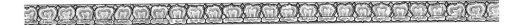

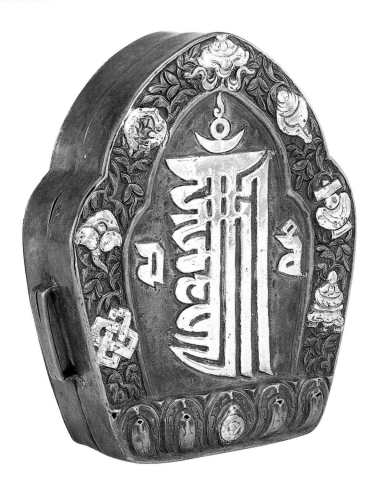

THE ALL-POWERFUL TEN

The group of letters known as the "All-Powerful Ten" is a *mantra* that is widely used in Tibetan decoration and often appears in low relief on the outside of wooden book covers. This powerful *mantra* is composed of the ten Sanskrit syllables OM HAM KSHA MA LA VA RA YA HUM PHAT and represents the cosmos as described in the *Kalachakra Tantra*, an important Buddhist text in Tibet. On this hammered copper amulet box (above), the syllables of the "All-Powerful Ten" are highlighted in silver (see also opposite in gold).

RECORDING THE *DHARMA*

After the Buddha passed away, a series of councils was held in order to collect his teachings and to codify the rules governing monastic life. This knowledge, collectively called the *dharma*, was first passed down by word of mouth, but the use of writing became inevitable as more and more commentaries and philosophical works based upon the *dharma* were composed.

The earliest Buddhist works are in a language generally referred to as Pali, closely related to Sanskrit and thought to have been spoken by the Buddha. Pali was the language used in the southern Buddhist tradition for writing commentaries and it is still used today in learned circles. However, in north India, Sanskrit—the "classical" language of ancient India—became the dominant literary medium and was used by the Mahayana and Vajrayana schools, the varieties of Buddhism that were carried into Tibet in the seventh century CE. The script used for the Tibetan language was also developed at this time, when King Songsten Gampo began sending envoys to India to study the art of writing and to create a system for transcribing the language. Tibetan script has changed little since.

Sanskrit learning was especially strong at Nalanda, the celebrated monastic university in eastern India, where many Tibetans went to study. Over several centuries, Sanskrit writings were translated into Tibetan, preserving texts that were subsequently lost in India. The Buddhist canon was systematically organized into one hundred and eight volumes by a Tibetan scholar, Bu-ston (1290–1364). By 1749, this body of literature, known as the *Kagyur*, had been translated into Mongolian—about a century after the Mongolian people had been converted to the Tibetan form of Buddhism.

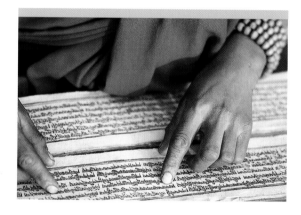

ABOVE **Tibetan books are long and narrow, with the words written horizontally across the face of each folio. There is no spine and the book is held together by a cord or string threaded through the middle of each page. This format, based on palm leaf originals, has been retained even for books produced on paper.**

RIGHT **A Tibetan monk sits reading Buddhist scriptures in the courtyard of the monastery at Langmusi in Gansu province, China. Until recently, the largest monasteries were the main centers of learning, and gifted monks underwent a rigorous educational training in all aspects of Buddhism and traditional knowledge.**

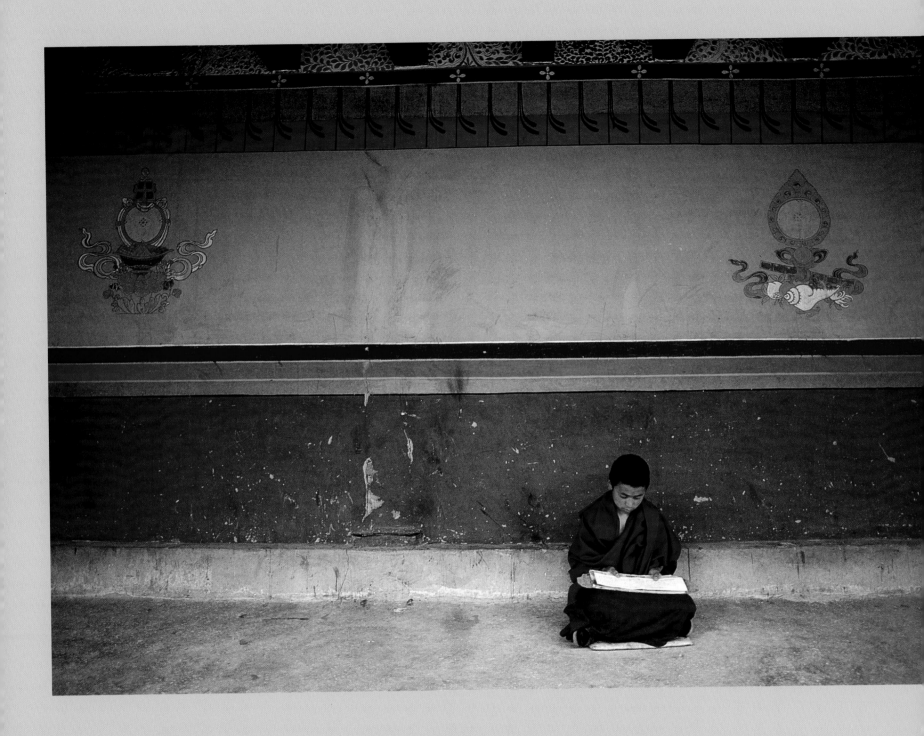

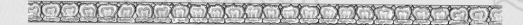

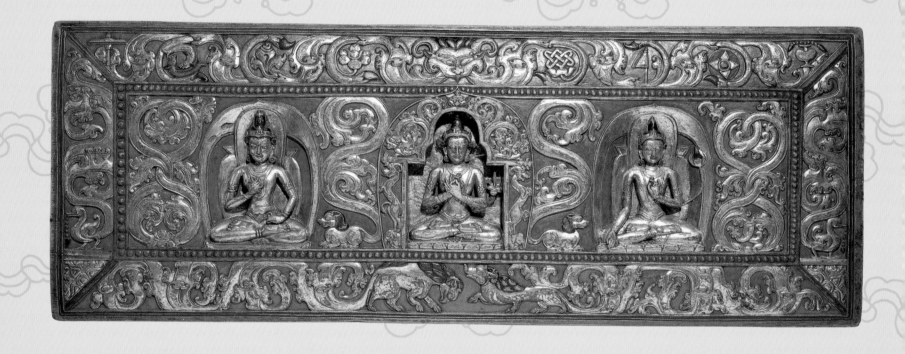

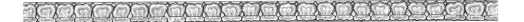

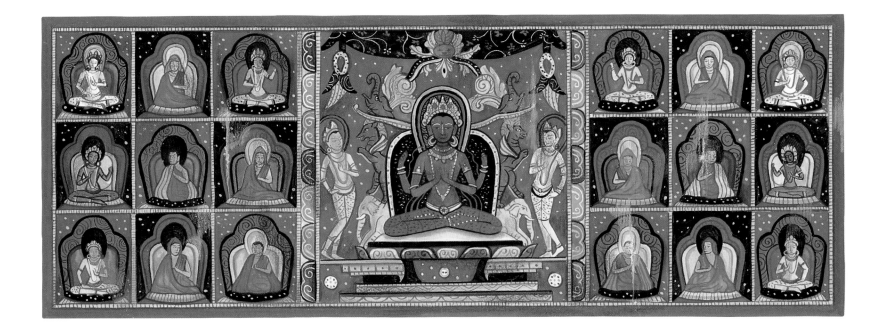

DECORATED BOOK COVERS

Book covers are one of the great art forms of Tibet. The wooden

boards that form the covers are carved with figures (often Buddhas,

as opposite), auspicious emblems, and scrollwork in low relief, and

then painted and gilded. The covers' inside surfaces are sometimes

painted with additional figures, such as those shown above.

PRAYER WHEELS AND BANNERS OF VICTORY

The prayer wheel (*mani 'khor-lo*) is a uniquely Tibetan spiritual device, employed by both monks and laypeople. Handheld prayer wheels have a metal drum which revolves on a pin; inside the drum are tightly rolled slips of paper printed with prayers, the most common being the formula *Om mani padme hum* (see page 68). Often, this popular *mantra* is also inscribed on the outside. Prayer wheels are set in motion by a flick of the wrist—with each spin the sacred texts within are understood as being read or chanted once. A prayer wheel can easily contain forty thousand *mantras*, and so, by Tibetan calculations, a few minutes of spinning will repeat the *mantras* millions of times. Because the most powerful invocations are those which are repeated mentally or quietly whispered, it follows that the silent turning of a prayer wheel is the most effective way of reciting *mantras*. It is the act of turning the wheel that brings religious merit and divine blessings—the devotee, the *mantra*, and the deity associated with the *mantra* are just parts of a mechanical ritual which is understood to radiate blessings into the environment.

Large prayer drums, sometimes several feet high and painted with *mantras* on the outside, are found in most Tibetan temples, where they are arranged in rows in a cloister. Devotees pass along the cloister, rotating each drum as they go. In some cases, prayer drums are turned by the wind or by running water. The perpetual turning of prayers in such drums is believed to fill the world with sacred invocations so that it is ever stable, ever renewed, and ever

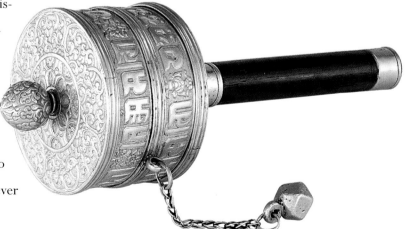

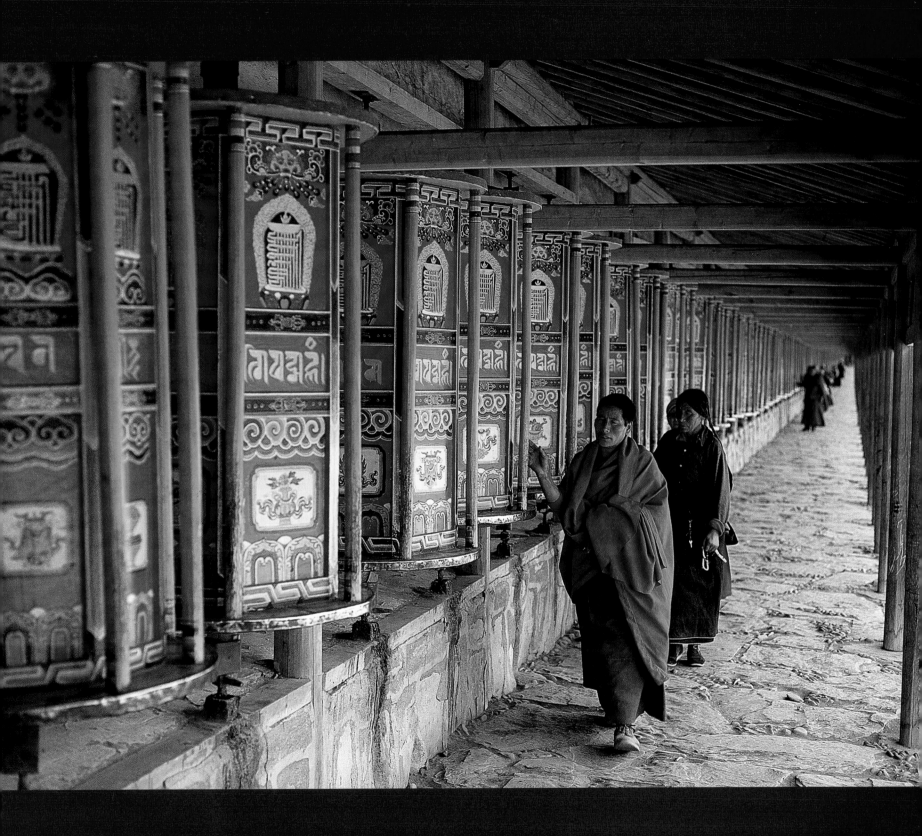

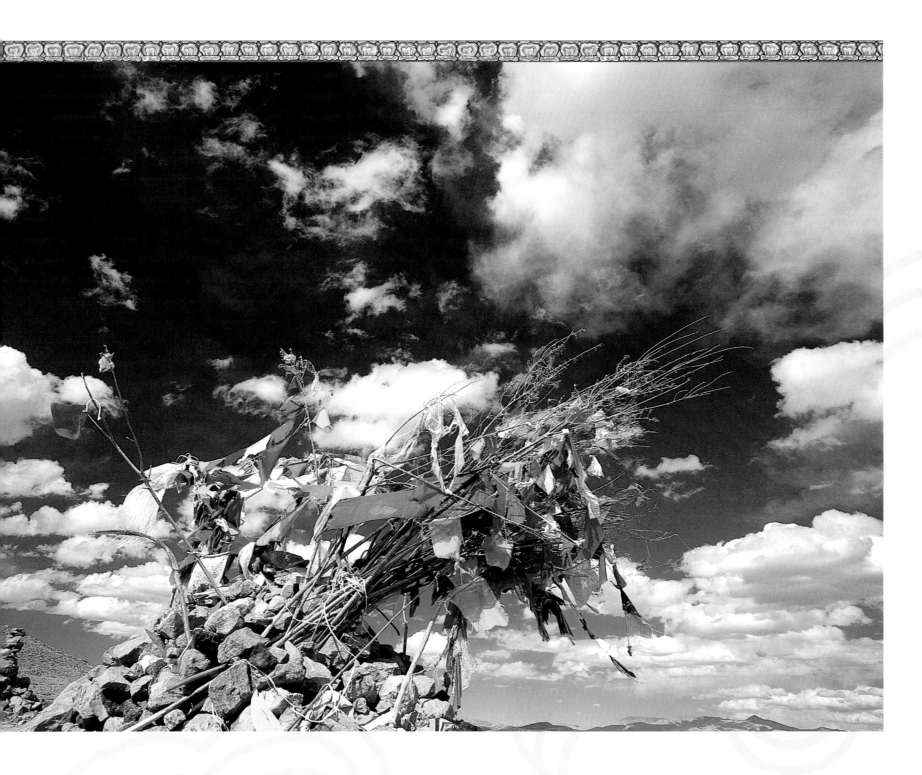

LEFT Flags and auspicious
banners are used through-
out the Buddhist world
as votive offerings. In
Tibet, they are frequently
raised on hilltops and
cairns in mountain passes,
such as this one between
Shigatse and Lhatse on
the Friendship Highway
between Lhasa and Nepal.

RIGHT This 9th-century
banner from the Buddhist
caves at Dunhuang in
central Asia carries an
image of the Bodhisattva
Vajra Pani. It has long
streamers and is closely
related in size and function
to the banners used in Tibet
during formal processions.

blessed for those on the path of enlightenment. The Buddha's teaching, the *dharma*, is considered perpetual and universal and is envisioned as a turning wheel, which is one of the eight auspicious emblems of Buddhism (see pages 100–101). Thus, the prayer wheels and prayer drums of Tibet, both in a literal and figurative sense, keep the wheel of the *dharma* rolling.

Prayer flags and banners serve a similar purpose to prayer wheels. They are positioned in prominent places, such as the rooftops of monasteries, and as they flutter in the breeze, the *mantras* and other blessings written upon them are believed to be freely distributed by the wind across the landscape. Most sets of flags are in five colors to symbolize the five elements of Tibetan tradition: earth, air, fire, water, and space. Some banners bear the eight auspicious emblems or protective animals, such as lions, dragons, and the eagle-headed Garuda (see page 57). Particularly large banners might be displayed during special ceremonies. The size of such banners—they were often so huge it would take dozens of people to unfurl them—endowed the images they bore with enormous spiritual power.

A particularly common device on flags is the "horse of the wind," or Lun-ta, a trotting steed carrying a precious stone surrounded by flames. This stone, known as the "radiant thought-gem" (*chinta-mani*), is believed to grant victory and all wishes. Prayer flags that depict Lun-ta are supposed to be especially effective.

Mountain passes are often marked by strings of prayer banners pinned to flagpoles and cairns. Travelers will always pause to add a stone to the cairn and attach a flag, which is sometimes little more than a strip of cloth. The prayers and *mantras* on prayer flags vary according to the particular deity on whom the devotee normally focuses his or her meditation. Those directed at the goddess Tara (see page 98) are especially commonplace on mountain flags, as she protects travelers from the dangers of the road.

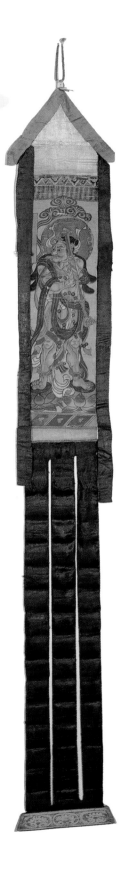

THE SACRED WORD

These are the opening pages of the *Prajna Paramita Sutra* ("Text of Transcendent Wisdom"), which is a section of the *Kagyur*, the comprehensive Tibetan anthology of Buddhist scripture. The text is written in gold on dark blue paper and, as with most high-quality Tibetan manuscripts, the opening leaves have silk flaps, which are folded over the face of the writing and miniatures when they are not in use to protect them from wear. The manuscript would once have been stored between wooden book covers (see page 76). The rectangular format is derived from the earliest Buddhist manuscripts, which were made of strips of palm leaf (see page 74).

This copy of the *Kagyur* was made and consecrated in the early eighteenth century by monks at the monastery of Shelkar near Dingri in southern Tibet. Built in 1266, the monastery was at first a Kagyu-pa establishment, but had come under the jurisdiction of the Gelug-pa school by the time this manuscript was made.

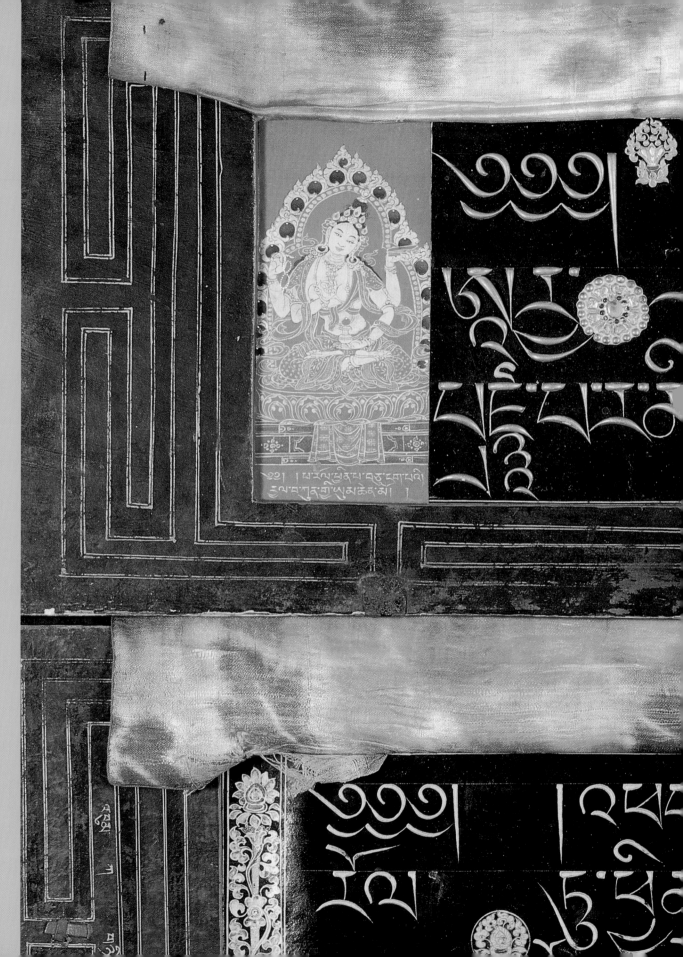

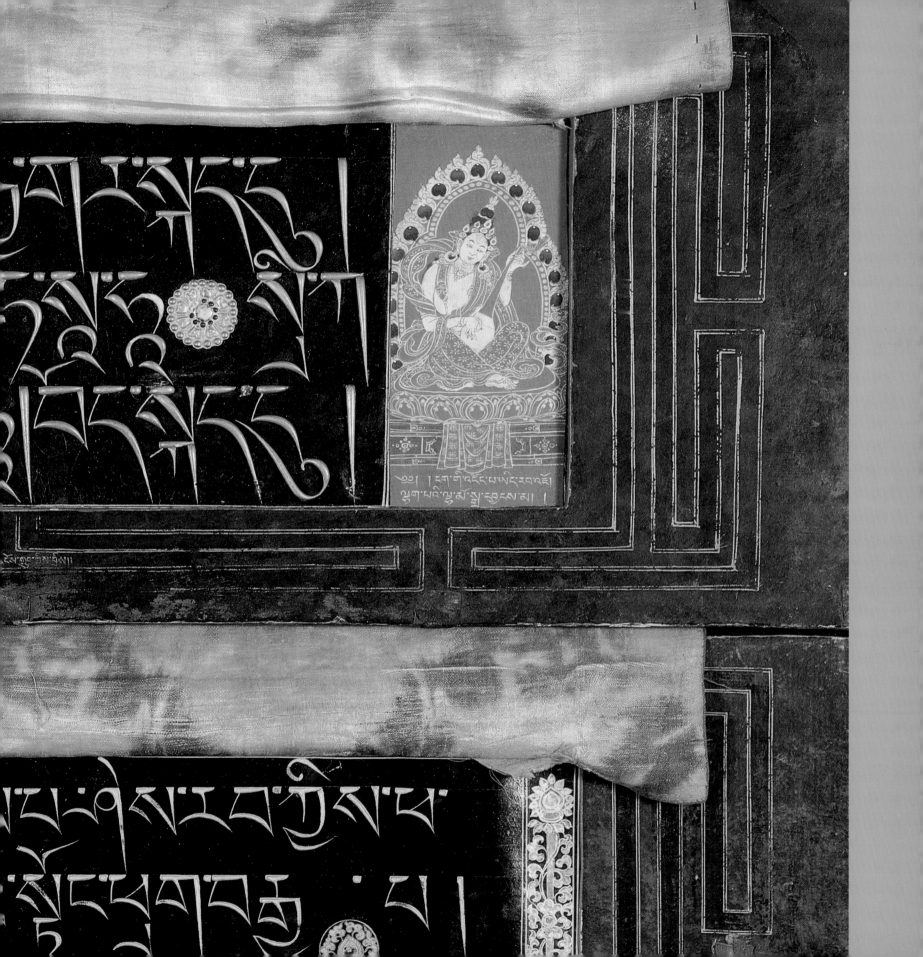

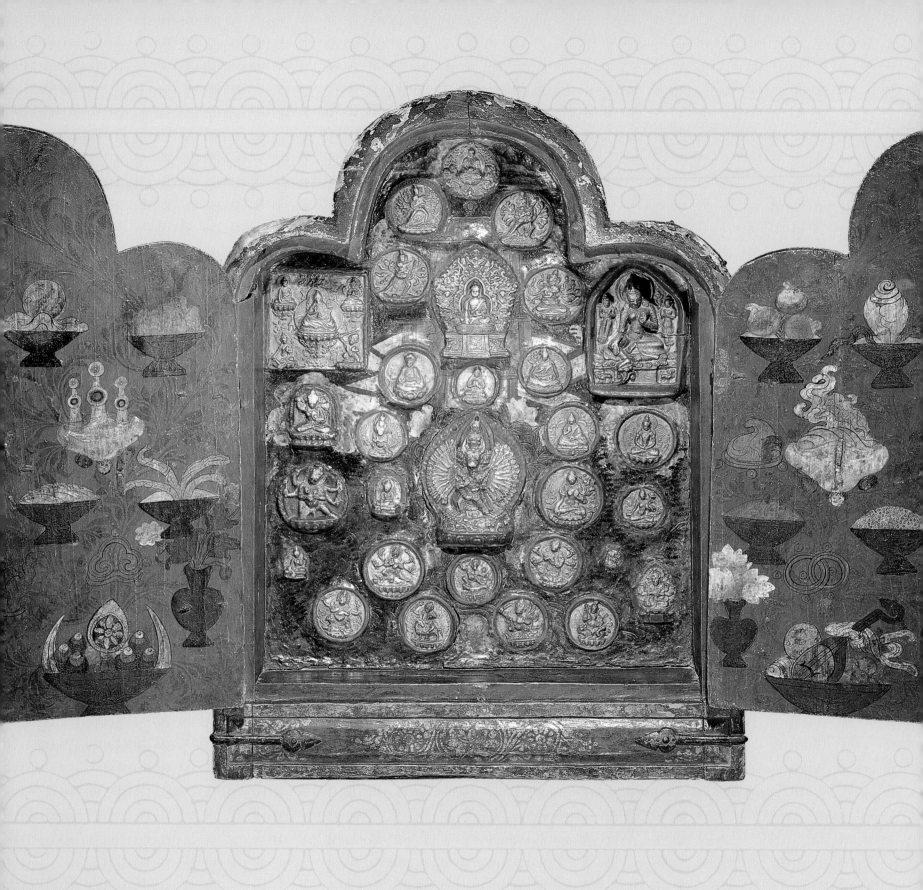

PERFECTED BEINGS, PERFECTED WORLDS

LEFT This portable wooden shrine contains votive plaques depicting the Buddha surrounded by various deities and *lama*s. Below the main Buddha is an image of Yamantaka Vajra Bhairava ("The Destroyer of Death"). The insides of the shrine's doors are decorated with representations of offerings.

The religious world of Tibet is inhabited by an elaborate pantheon of gods and goddesses, guardian deities, local spirits, saints, incarnations, teachers, philosophers, and wonder-workers. Most of the gods and goddesses were part of the Indian traditions of Mahayana Buddhism, but new forms were added as a result of the visionary meditations experienced by the great saints and *lama*s. When a deity appeared in a new or variant form, the vision and the means of summoning it were recorded so that it could be passed on in the *lama*'s spiritual tradition. The Tibetan pantheon is thus not rigid and systematic, but an organic view of religious reality which varies according to school and location.

BELOW The outer doors of the 19th-century wooden shrine shown opposite are painted with delicate floral motifs.

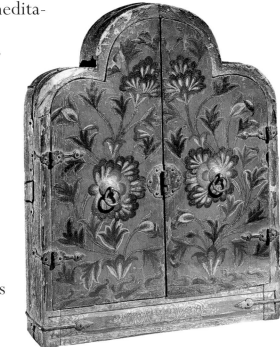

THE COSMIC BUDDHAS

Tibetan Buddhism is an outwardly polytheistic religion, with numerous divinities and other supernatural beings. But it is underpinned by an uncompromising belief that all the gods belong to the world of phenomena and are thus—like all things—subject to change, death, and reincarnation. In contrast, the supreme truth is immortal, unchanging, absolute, and eternal. This ultimate Truth is known as the Adi Buddha, or "Primordial Buddha." His essence is said to be "pure consciousness," the same consciousness that lies at the heart of all individuals. For this reason, everyone is thought to have a gateway to Adi Buddha, the ultimate reality, within themselves.

Tibetan Buddhism has a range of religious techniques and rites (*sadhanas*) to guide individuals toward the Truth. The knowledge of these techniques, their application and the way they are to be transmitted to the next generation is controlled by the various Tibetan Buddhist schools and spiritual lineages. Over their long histories, these schools have developed differing visions of Adi Buddha.

The Nyingma-pa school describes Adi Buddha as Samanta Bhadra ("Entirely Auspicious"); for the Kadam-pa, the supreme reality is Vajra Sattva ("Diamond Being"); while the Gelug-pa view Adi Buddha as Vajra Dhara ("Holder of the Diamond").

Although Samanta Bhadra, Vajra Sattva, and Vajra Dhara are conceived as deities, they are not competing gods but rather different aspects of, or approaches to, the supreme being. Both Vajra Sattva and Vajra Dhara are depicted holding the diamond *vajra*, or thunderbolt, an emblem of the indestructibility of *sunyata*—the name given by Buddhists to the imperishable "final state" of reality, which is not bound up with existence.

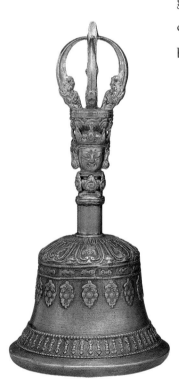

BELOW As symbols of wisdom and compassion, the bell (*ghanta*) and the pronged thunderbolt (*vajra*), such as these bronze examples, are key implements in Tibetan Buddhist ritual and meditation.

RIGHT This 18th- or 19th-century *thangka* painting portrays the cosmic Buddha Vajra Sattva. Seated on a cloud above an idyllic mountainscape, he holds a bell and thunderbolt and has multicolored halos emanating from his head and body.

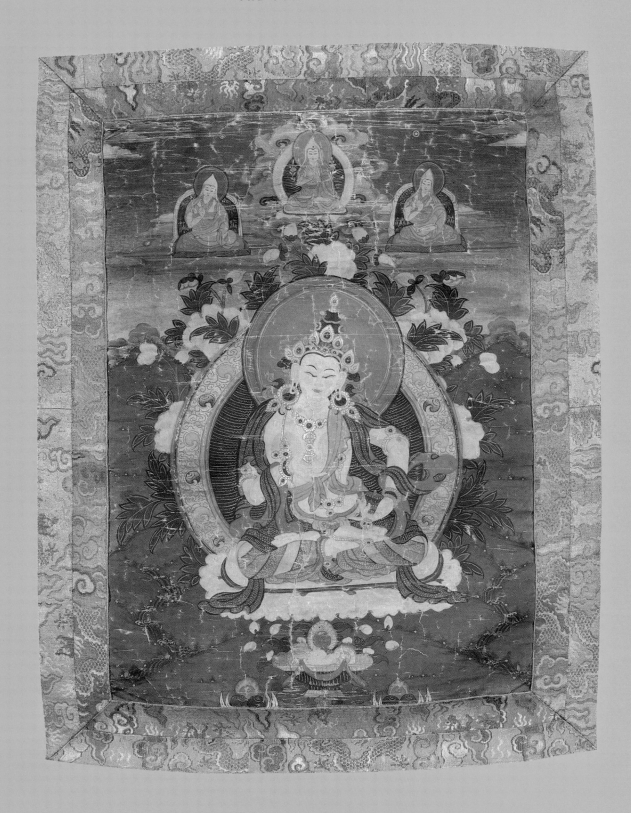

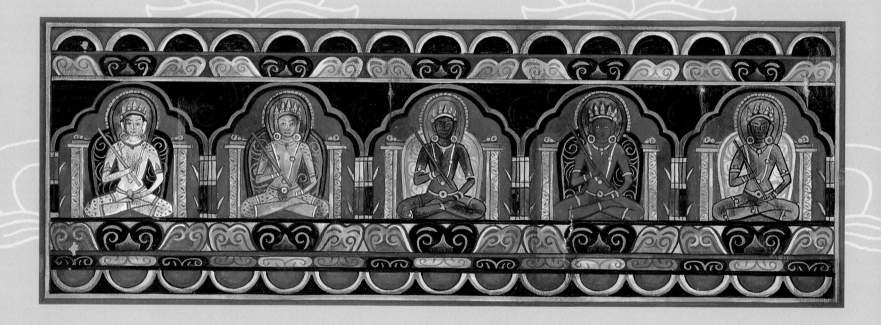

Vairochana   **Ratnasambhava**   **Amoghasiddhi**   **Amitabha (Amitayus)**   **Akshobhya**

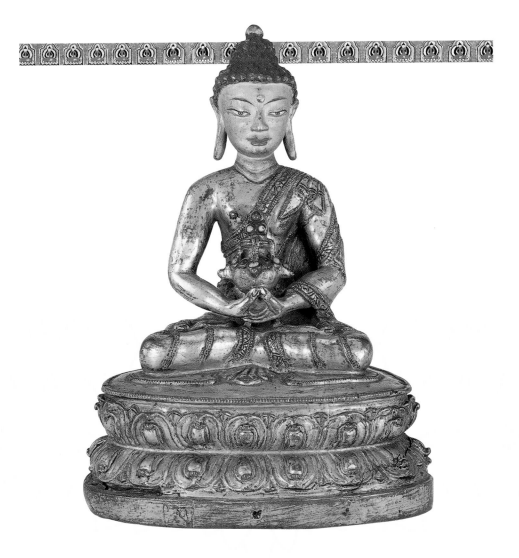

A GALLERY OF BUDDHAS

In the Tibetan Buddhist pantheon, the primordial Buddha is
surrounded by five celestial Buddhas (see opposite), who represent
his various divine attributes. The most popular of these is Amitabha,
who also appears as Amitayus, the "Buddha of Infinite Life."
Amitayus is usually portrayed, as above, holding a pot containing the
elixir of immortality. The five celestial Buddhas are linked to the five
elements, the five senses, and the five key energy centers in the
human body, located in the head, mouth, heart, navel, and feet.

TEMPLES OF THE *DHARMA*: ALCHI

In the steep upper valleys of the Indus River, not far from Leh in northern India, is the Ladakh Buddhist monastery at Alchi. The temples in the monastery are the most important early monuments in the western Himalayas, magnificent reminders of the time of the "Second Propagation" of Buddhism in Tibet (see page 18).

Little is known about the history of Alchi— there are no written records referring to the monastery, except for a few inscriptions attesting that the Sumtsek, the oldest of its temples, was founded by a monk named Tshultrim-O ca. 1200CE. Alchi is renowned for its wall paintings of the Mahayana pantheon, which have remained virtually unchanged for the last eight centuries. Alchi also features important early woodwork, as the carved door frame shown here attests. The door (an entrance to one of the shrines) has six receding jambs, each richly carved with a variety of floral motifs and Buddhist figures, including, in the center at the top, the figure of a Garuda (a protector against malevolent forces). The design is based directly on doors that once graced temples in northern India, but the turbulent history of the Indian plains has meant that only a few stone fragments of these temples have survived.

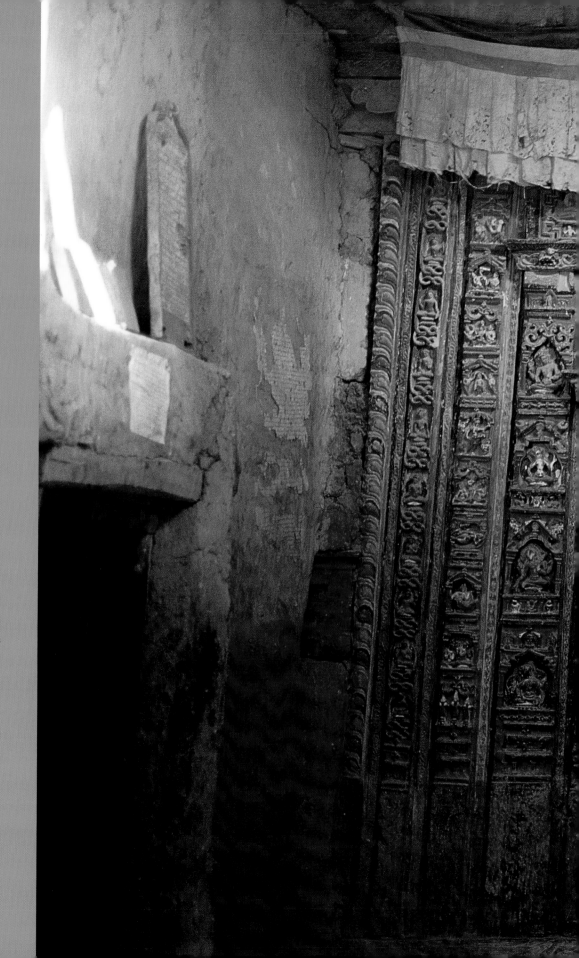

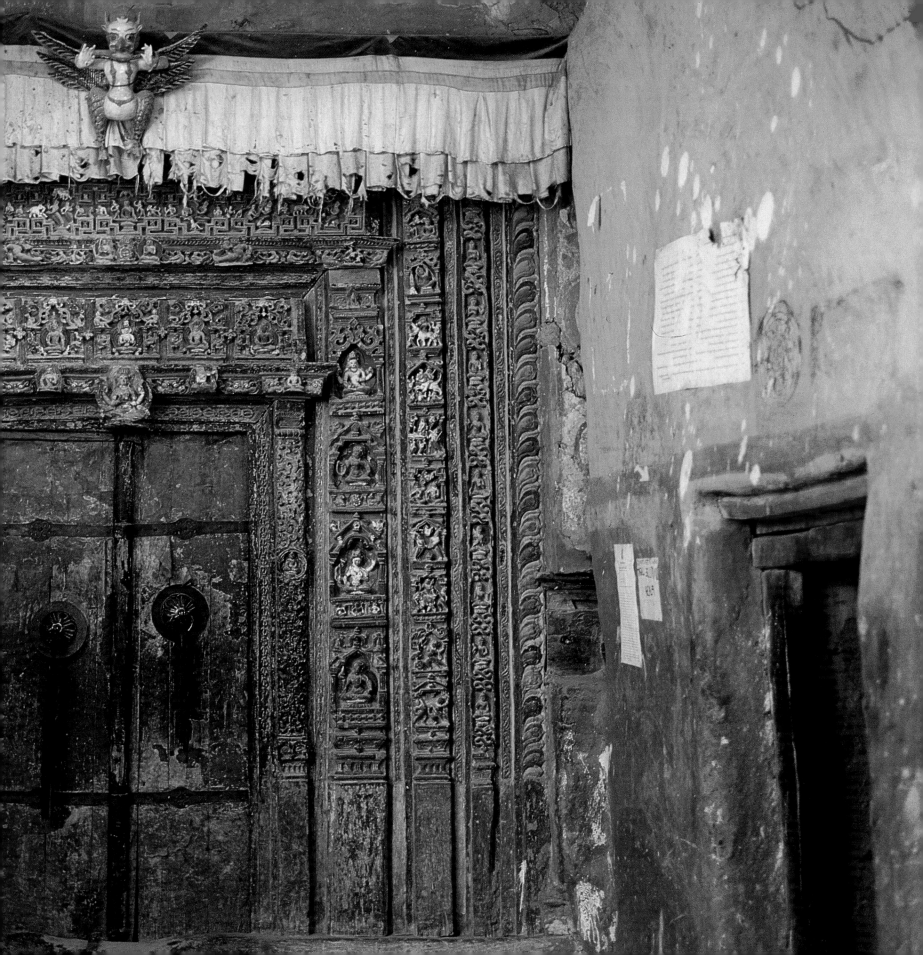

COMPASSIONATE HEROES

The Adi Buddha is immutable and passive like the Celestial Buddhas who surround him (see page 89). In Tibetan belief, it is the Bodhisattvas who are the active creators of the universe. A Bodhisattva (literally "One whose Essence is Supreme Knowledge") is a perfect being, who heroically delays final liberation or enlightenment in order to help others gain salvation. Five of these Bodhisattvas, who hold the emblems of the Celestial Buddhas and are understood to be direct emanations of them, are Chakra Pani ("Wheel Bearer"), Vajra Pani ("Thunderbolt Bearer"), Ratna Pani ("Jewel Bearer"), Padma Pani ("Lotus Bearer"), and Vishva Pani ("Double-thunderbolt Bearer").

Among the more widely worshiped Bodhisattvas in Tibet are Avalokiteshvara, Manjushri, and Maitreya. The most popular Bodhisattva of all is Avalokiteshvara, the "Lord of Compassion" and the patron deity of Tibet, who is believed to be reincarnated in every Dalai Lama. His name literally means "The Lord who Looks Down," that is, he looks down with compassion on the suffering of the world. In one text, the *Karandavyuha* ("Jewel-box Display"), Avalokiteshvara is described as taking a vow to descend into the realm of Yama, the Lord of Death. Waters miraculously began to flow from the Bodhisattva's fingers to cool the molten iron and flames of hell. Like all Bodhisattvas, Avalokiteshvara has many forms, but he can often be recognized by a small figure of the Buddha Amitabha, his spiritual father, which is inserted like a talisman in his hair or crown. The Bodhisattva's eleven-headed form, Arya Avalokiteshvara, also appears frequently in Tibet (see pages 96–97). The deep attachment of the

LEFT This 12th-century figure of Manjushri, cast in bronze and inlaid with silver, copper, and colored stones, shows the Bodhisattva holding a book and sword, the attributes with which he is most commonly depicted. Like Avalokiteshvara, Manjushri is believed to be an emanation of the Buddha Amitabha.

RIGHT Avalokiteshvara is portrayed seated in his celestial palace on Mount Potalaka in this 18th- or 19th-century *thangka* painting. Avalokiteshvara is an emanation of the celestial Buddha Amitabha, who appears at the top of the painting in his own palatial enclosure.

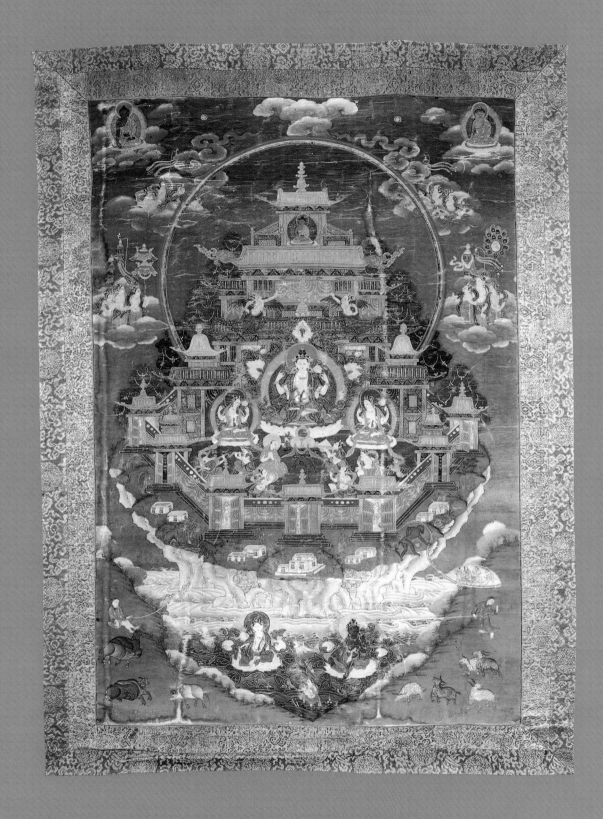

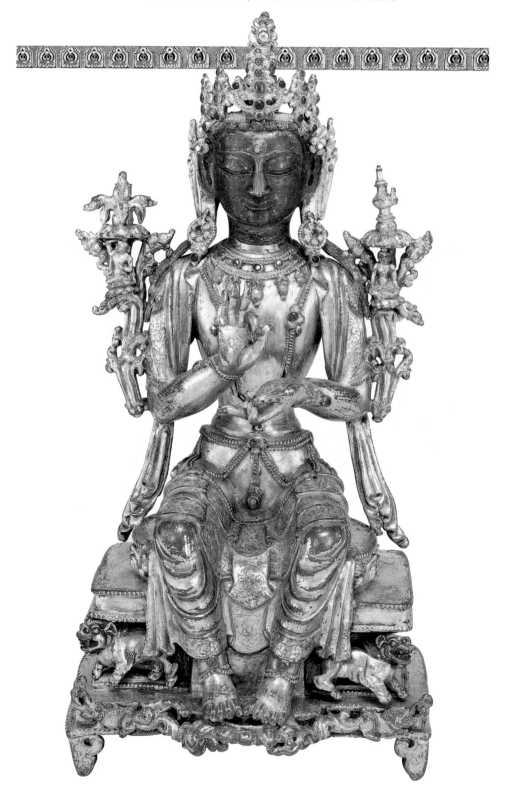

Tibetan people to this Bodhisattva is illustrated by legends describing how the very first Tibetans were the children of a fierce mountain goddess and a monkey who was an emanation of Avalokiteshvara.

Manjushri, the personification of transcendent wisdom, is regarded as an offspring of the Buddha Amitabha or Akshobhaya. He has many forms, but often wields the "sword of discrimination," a weapon with which he is said to cut the roots of ignorance (see illustration, page 92). By worshiping him, devotees enrich their wisdom, develop a more retentive memory, and enhance their eloquence and their ability to master sacred scripture. For this reason, in addition to his sword, Manjushri holds a palm leaf manuscript, traditionally the *Prajna Paramita Sutra* ("Text of Transcendent Wisdom"). Because of this connection with sacred knowledge, Manjushri is often represented on book covers (see page 76). In the fourteenth century CE, Manjushri is said to have incarnated himself in Tsong Khapa, Tibet's greatest monk-scholar, whose extraordinary life and work laid the foundation for the Gelug-pa order.

Maitreya ("Loving One") is the name given to the Bodhisattva who is yet to come. It is believed that he now resides in a paradise called the Tushita heaven and is waiting for the time when he will descend to earth as the next human Buddha and reestablish the *dharma* in all its purity.

The celebrated sage Asanga—a sixth-century CE master—is said to have visited Maitreya in the Tushita heaven using the exceptional powers he acquired during a sixteen-year period of intense meditation retreat. Asanga received instruction in philosophical matters and transcribed these points in what are known as "the Five Works of Maitreya."

LEFT **Tibetan Buddhists believe that Maitreya, the Bodhisattva of the future, will incarnate himself on earth and reestablish the truth of the Buddha's doctrine. His emblems are the white campa flower and, more especially, the water pot. Both are shown on lotus stalks beside his shoulders in this 19th-century gilded bronze statuette inlaid with precious stones.**

BELOW **This 16th- to 18th-century water vessel was used for sprinkling holy water, a feature of many Tibetan rituals. The same type of vessel appears as Maitreya's emblem beside his left shoulder in the representation that is shown opposite.**

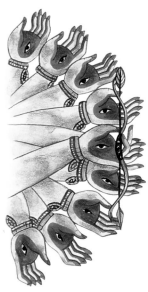

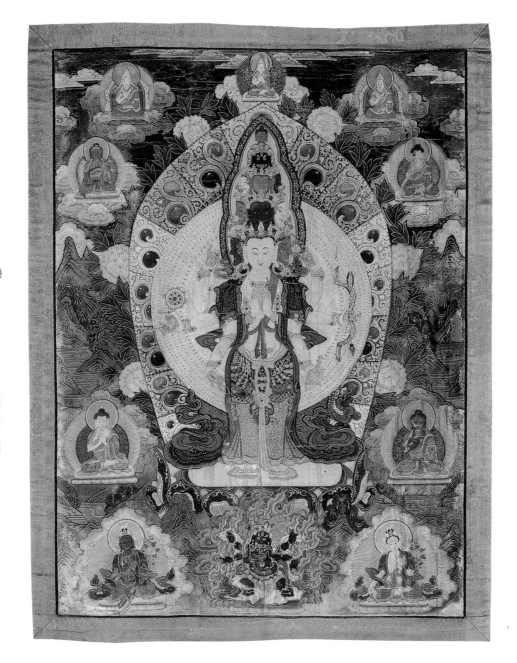

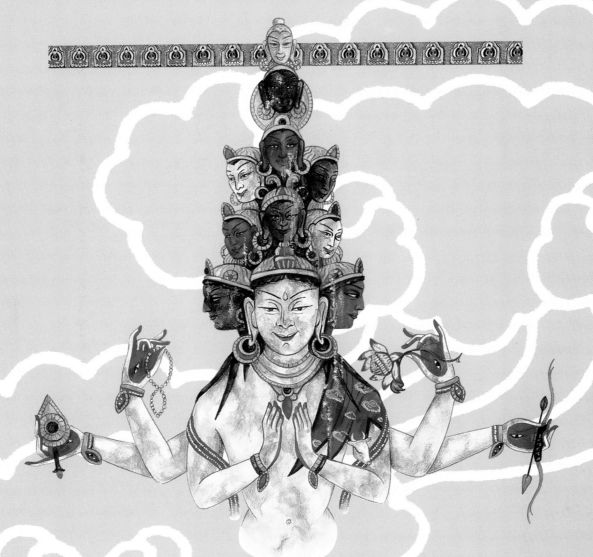

AVALOKITESHVARA, THE MANY-ARMED LORD

Known as Arya Avalokiteshvara, the eleven-headed, multiarmed form of the great Bodhisattva (see above and at the center of the *thangka* painting opposite) first appeared in western India in the sixth century CE. One of the explanations for his eleven heads is that, because space is traditionally defined as having ten directions, ten of the heads symbolize Avalokiteshvara's all-seeing dominion over the universe. The eleventh head, at the top, is that of Amitabha (see page 89), the celestial Buddha of which Avalokiteshvara is a manifestation.

GODDESSES OF WISDOM

The great goddess of Wisdom manifests herself in twenty-one forms, the most common of which are the Green Tara and the White Tara. They are traditionally described as being born from the tears shed by the Bodhisattva Avalokiteshvara, who wept to see the extent of suffering in the world. From his tears sprang lotus flowers from which the Taras were born. As goddesses of divine energy and transcendent wisdom, they gave Avalokiteshvara the courage to continue in his impossible task of delivering all beings from suffering.

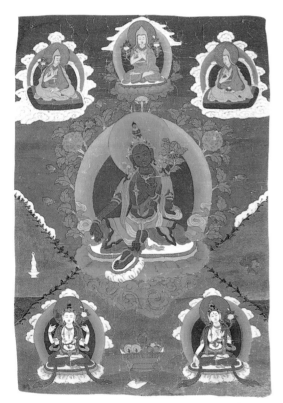

The Taras are divine saviors and help deal with everyday dangers. For example, the *Sadhana Mala* ("Garland of Meditative Techniques") states that the worship of Green Tara will deliver one from the "eight great perils," which are generally taken to be fire, water, lions, elephants, imprisonment, snakes, thieves, and disease caused by evil spirits. White Tara, in contrast, offers serenity, prosperity, health, and good fortune.

When Buddhism was first introduced into Tibet, the Taras were believed to have incarnated themselves in the wives of King Songtsen Gampo—Green Tara incarnating as the Nepalese queen and White Tara as the Chinese queen. Tara was also the tutelary deity of Atisha, the Buddhist master who came to Tibet from India in 1042, and since that time, the goddess has enjoyed a wide Tibetan following. Her most distinguished devotee was the first Dalai Lama (1391–1474), who composed verses in her praise. It is believed that the faithful can appeal directly to Tara without the intermediary of a master or *lama* and statues of her are found on virtually all Tibetan domestic altars.

LEFT In this *thangka* painting, Green Tara is flanked by Tsong Khapa (top, center) and two other *lamas*; below are White Tara and Avalokiteshvara.

RIGHT With her right hand, Tara makes the gesture of granting boons (*varada mudra*) in this 19th-century statuette. The eyes in her palms, the soles of her feet, and her forehead signify her ability to see suffering in every corner of the world.

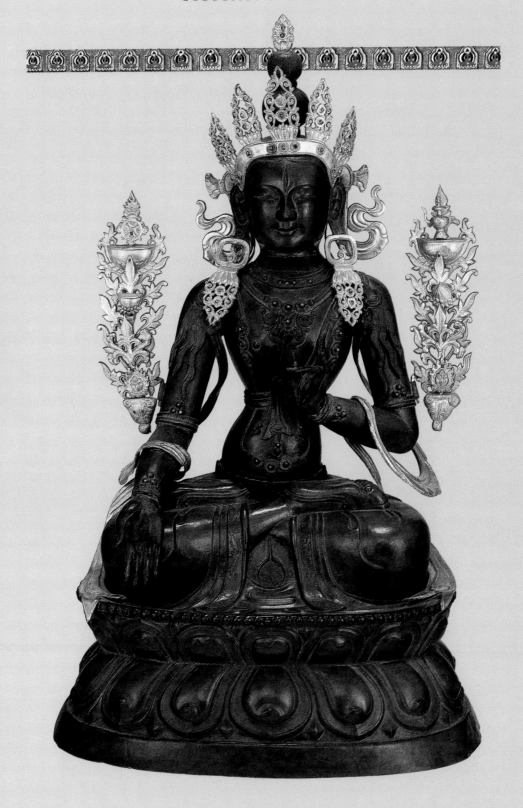

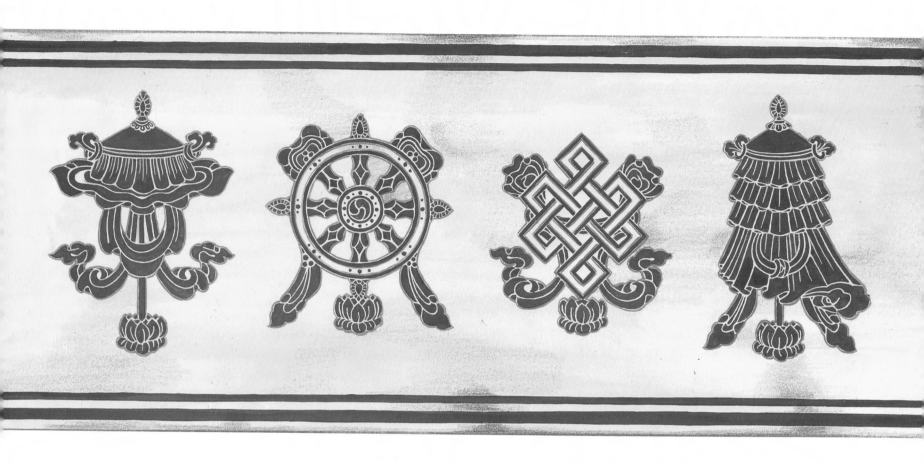

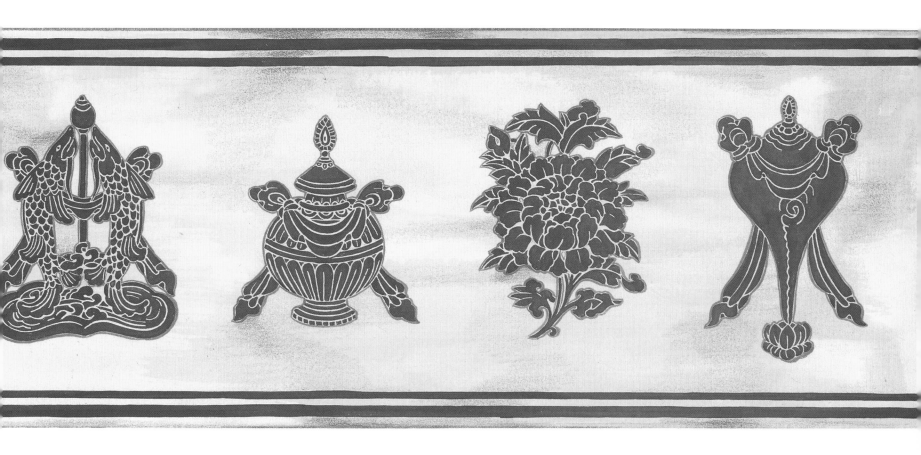

AUSPICIOUS EMBLEMS

Eight auspicious motifs frequently appear in Tibetan art (above, left to right): the "royal parasol" is emblematic of the Buddha and his heroic pursuit of enlightenment; the eight-spoked wheel represents the Buddha's *dharma*; the endless knot symbolizes the inescapable nature of worldly existence; the "victory banner" stands on Mount Meru in the center of the Buddhist universe; the two fishes symbolize happiness and utility; the vase represents plenty; the lotus denotes purity; and the conch shell, because it grows in a clockwise direction, is symbolic of turning to the right, that is, turning toward the *dharma*.

THE UNION OF WISDOM
AND COMPASSION

In his *Mahayana Sutralankara* ("Embellished Sutras of Mahayana"), the sixth-century sage Asanga gave a famous critique of the southern school of Buddhism, stating that it focused too narrowly on individual liberation from the cycle of birth, death, and rebirth. This is a key difference between the Theravada Buddhism of Sri Lanka, Burma, and Thailand, and the Mahayana of north India, Tibet, and east Asia. While both affirm that liberation, or enlightenment, is the final destination of the human soul, Mahayana emphasizes that an individual's pursuit of liberation must be tempered by a deep sympathy for all other living beings. Thus the ideal figure in Theravada is the enlightened monastic saint (Arhat), who has attained supreme wisdom, yet remains entirely detached, while in Mahayana it is the perfect, yet infinitely compassionate, heavenly savior (Bodhisattva).

In Mahayana, both wisdom (*prajna* or *sunyata*) and compassion (*upaya* or *karuna*) are essential components of spiritual life. The abstract qualities of *prajna* and *karuna* are considered as female and male respectively, and their perfect union is visualized as a goddess and a god in sexual embrace (*yab-yum*).

Wisdom without compassion can achieve nothing because it is inert; compassion uninformed by wisdom is easily over-whelmed by suffering. The ultimate goal of enlightenment entails a combination of these opposites, a goal achieved, in the Mahayana view, by a slow ripening of the necessary "perfections" over many lives and incarnations. The Tantric

RIGHT This deity is Yamantaka Vajra Bhairava, the "Destroyer of Death" and "Diamond Terrifier." A manifestation of Manjushri (the Bodhisattva of wisdom) and tutelary deity of the Gelug-pa school, he is shown in union with his consort Vajra Vetali. An inscription on the reverse gives the name of the individual who donated the figure to a Tibetan Buddhist temple in Beijing. The inscription is dated to the reign of the Chinese emperor Jiaqing (1796–1820).

RIGHT The central figure in this 18th-century *thangka* painting is Samanta Bhadra, depicted in union with his "wisdom partner" (*shakti*). They are surrounded by images of Buddhas, saints, and *lama*s.

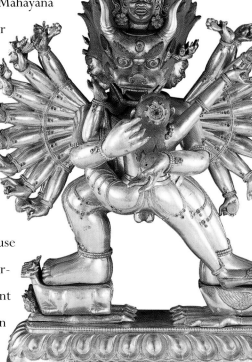

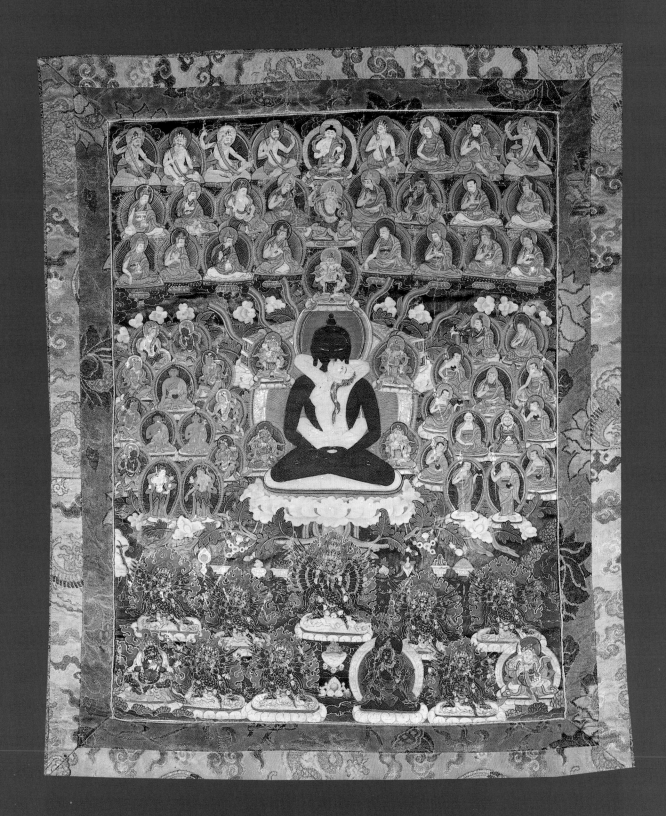

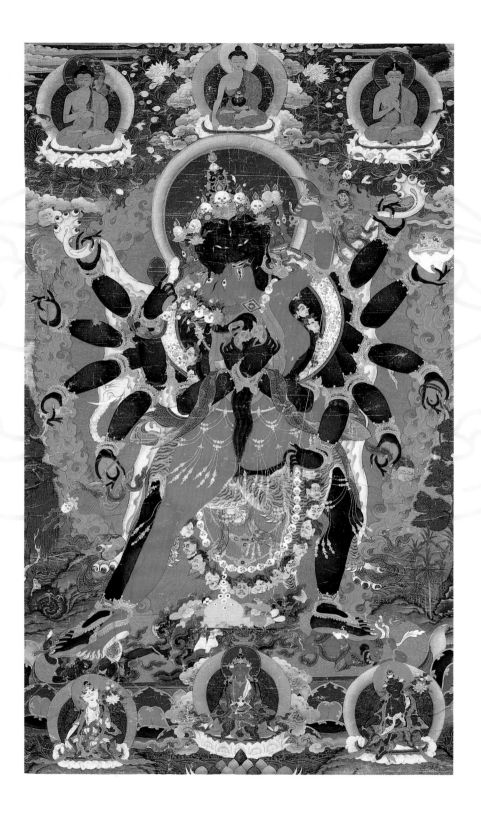

LEFT **This *thangka* shows the tutelary deity (*yi-dam*) Chakra Samvara in union with his "wisdom partner" Vajra Varahi.**

Buddhist tradition of Vajrayana (the "Vehicle of the Diamantine Thunderbolt") accepts the Mahayana interpretation but asserts that individuals can achieve full enlightenment in just one lifetime. This is believed to be possible through the vigorous application of a variety of powerful techniques, passed down in the master-to-disciple lineages of Tibet. In many cases these techniques are said to have been revealed directly to the Great Adepts of India by the goddess Vajra Varahi in her mountain retreat at Kailas, where she is the divine consort of Chakra Samvara, the esoteric manifestation of the historical Buddha. The techniques involve the making and contemplation of *mandala* diagrams (see pages 34–37), fasting and other penance, and the use of prayers and *mantra*s in meditation and in the performance of rituals. These are collectively designed to unlock the powers hidden within, unfolding the ocean of wisdom and compassion that are believed to lie in the depths of the human heart.

The techniques, deities, and texts of the Vajrayana tradition are often described as Tantra or Tantric, terms popularly associated with orgiastic rites and images of deities in sexual union. The term Tantra is more correctly a description of the comprehensive system of speculative thought which explains how to pursue enlightenment and provides a full range of yogic and meditative techniques to enable the devotee to achieve this end.

While sexual acts of a ritualized nature may have been performed by the Great Adepts and their early followers in the process of divine visualization, in the later Tibetan tradition, certainly from the time of the great Indian sage Atisha (see page 108), such acts are conceived and performed in entirely symbolic ways.

LEFT **The supreme Buddha, according to the Gelug-pa school, is Vajra Dhara. In this image, he holds a bell and thunderbolt (*vajra*) and embraces his "wisdom partner" (*shakti*), who holds a skull cup and dagger.**

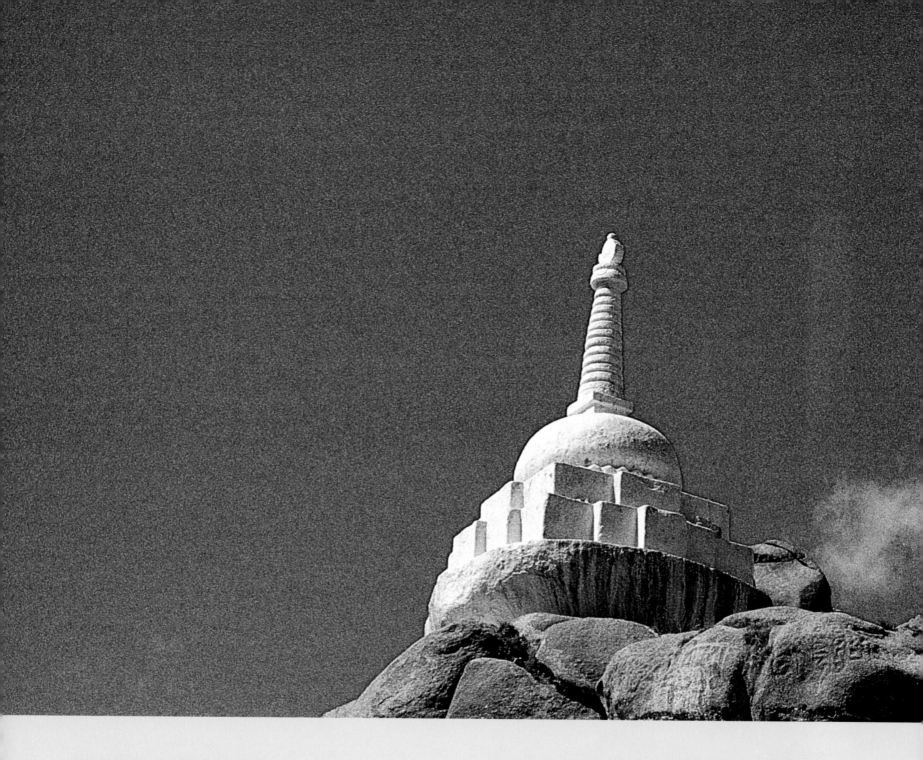

THE WAY OF A TANTRIC MASTER

When Padmasambhava was summoned to Tibet by King Trisong Detsen to help establish the Buddhist monastery at Samye (see pages 40–41), he first met the ruler near the Tsangpo River at Zurkhardo. A series of *stupa*s were built on the hills there to commemorate this historic meeting of Tantric master and all-powerful king. The *stupa*s are visible for many miles along the Tsangpo, marking the river crossing and traditional pilgrim route to nearby Samye. Zurkhardo

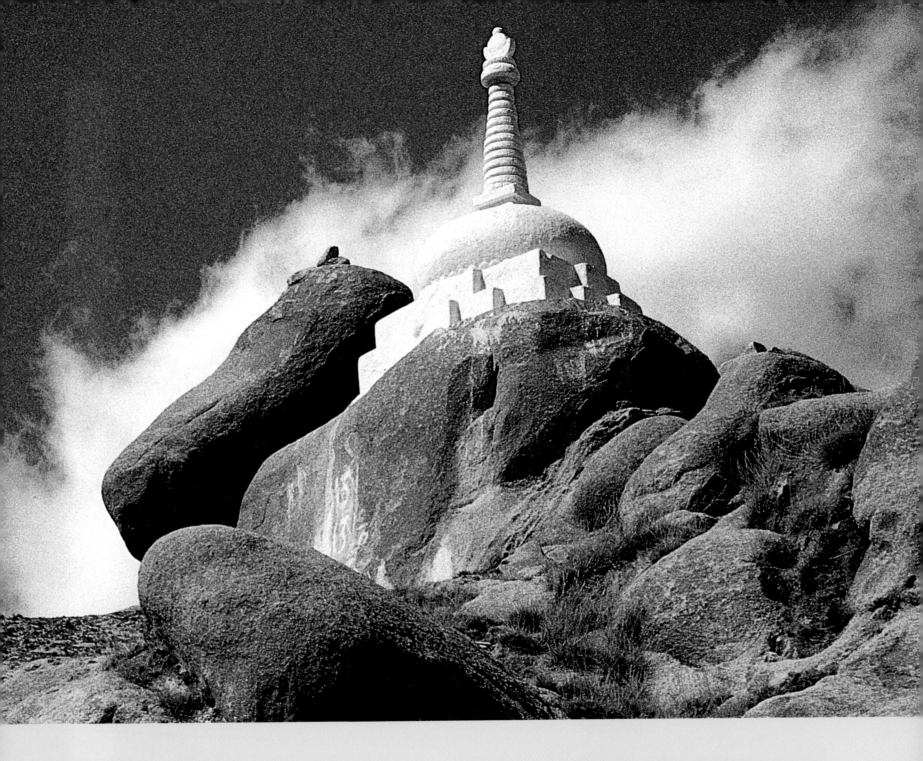

recalls the "Invitation Rock" at Mihintale in Sri Lanka where, more than nine centuries before the time of Padmasambhava, the Buddhist elder Mahinda met King Devanampiya Tissa. Just as the early Buddhists had to overcome a local cult of nature spirits (*yakkha*) in Sri Lanka, so Padmasambhava is said to have faced the ancient gods of Tibet at Mount Hepori, a sacred hill overlooking Samye and a seat of power for the Bon deities worshiped by the old aristocratic families of central Tibet.

SAINTS AND SAGES

BELOW Atisha was one of
the key figures in the re-
establishment of Buddhism
in Tibet during the 11th
century. This 19th-century
statue shows him with a
round basket containing
the Buddhist scriptures,
and a *chorten* (see page 46).

The special character and strength of Tibetan Buddhism owes much to the devout Tibetans who undertook the long and perilous journey to India in search of holy texts and great religious teachers. In the late tenth century CE, a leading figure in the effort to establish the *dharma* in Tibet was Rinchen Zangpo, who traveled to India under the patronage of Yeshe-o, king of Gu-ge in western Tibet. After almost twenty years abroad, Rinchen became an active teacher and translator in his homeland at Toling, where he constructed religious buildings from 1014.

King Yeshe-o was determined that Buddhism should be properly established in Tibet and repeatedly issued invitations to Atisha, the foremost Indian sage of the day. Atisha was fully conversant with all eighteen philosophical schools of Buddhism and, according to Ratnakara, the abbot of the monastic university of Vikramashila, "held in his hand the keys to all the monasteries of India." Initially reluctant to leave his homeland, Atisha was finally persuaded to make a short visit, arriving in Tibet in 1042. Atisha was a powerful reformer who placed great emphasis on monastic discipline, and his chief pupil, Dromton, established the Kadam-pa school of Tibetan Buddhism after Atisha died in 1054.

Shortly after Atisha's death, Marpa, who was a farmer from central Tibet, made three journeys to eastern India. He studied with a variety of masters, the most important being Naropa, a Great Adept and the preeminent Buddhist mystic of the eleventh century. On his return, Marpa gained many followers, including Milarepa (see page 50), whose disciples in turn established the Kargyu-pa school.

RIGHT This *thangka*
painting, which dates from
the 18th or 19th century,
shows Saraha, an arrow-
maker who became a
Great Adept (*Mahasiddha*).
He appears with his pupil
Nagarjuna (top left) and
the scholar Bu-ston (1290–
1364), who sits holding
a book on his lap. The
other figures are also Great
Adepts, among them Virupa
(top right) and Dombi
Heruka (bottom left).

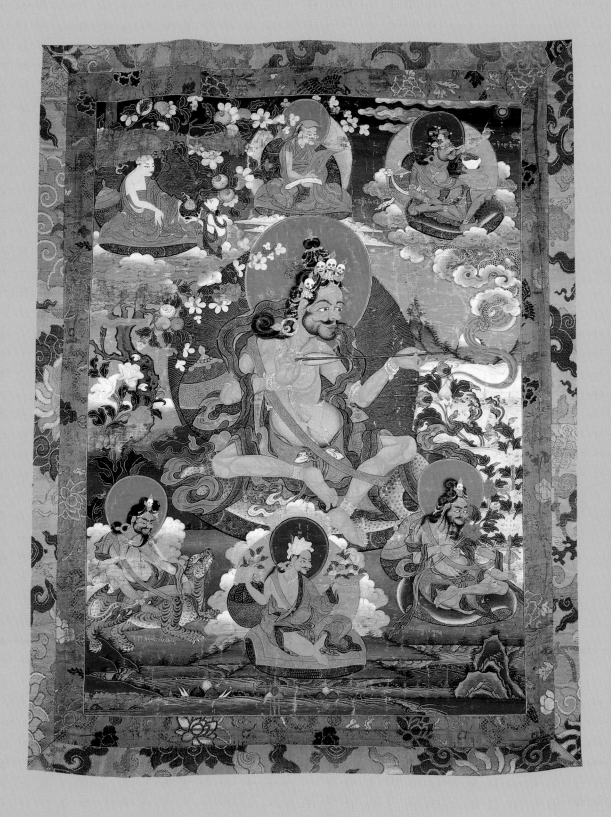

RESTING PLACE OF A SAINT

Atisha, the greatest Buddhist teacher of the eleventh century, came to Tibet from eastern India in 1042 at the age of sixty. After visiting the western kingdom of Gu-ge, he traveled to central Tibet and finally settled at Nyetang, around 17 miles (28km) southwest of Lhasa. Atisha died at Nyetang in 1054 and the temple complex known as Dolma Lhakhang (the central court of which is shown here) contains many personal items, including his bodily relics, begging bowl, books, and some of the sacred images he brought from India.

Atisha was especially devoted to Tara (see page 98). The shrine at Nyetang contains twenty-one Taras, given to the temple in the seventeenth century. Atisha's original sculpture of the goddess is now missing but it is believed to have been a miraculous image endowed with the power of speech. The Nyetang temple also has a *thangka* of Maha Kala, a popular protector deity (see page 122), that is said to have been painted using some of Atisha's blood. Another relic of great sanctity is the skull of Naropa, the Great Adept with whom Marpa studied (see page 50).

Atisha's enormous influence owes much to the fact that he learned Tibetan, a language seldom studied by early Buddhist scholars in India. A key feature of Atisha's teaching was his emphasis on the absolute devotion that a disciple must have for his master—only those who had made a complete and uncompromising commitment to their spiritual *lama*s were worthy of receiving the higher truths which could bring them to enlightenment in a single lifetime.

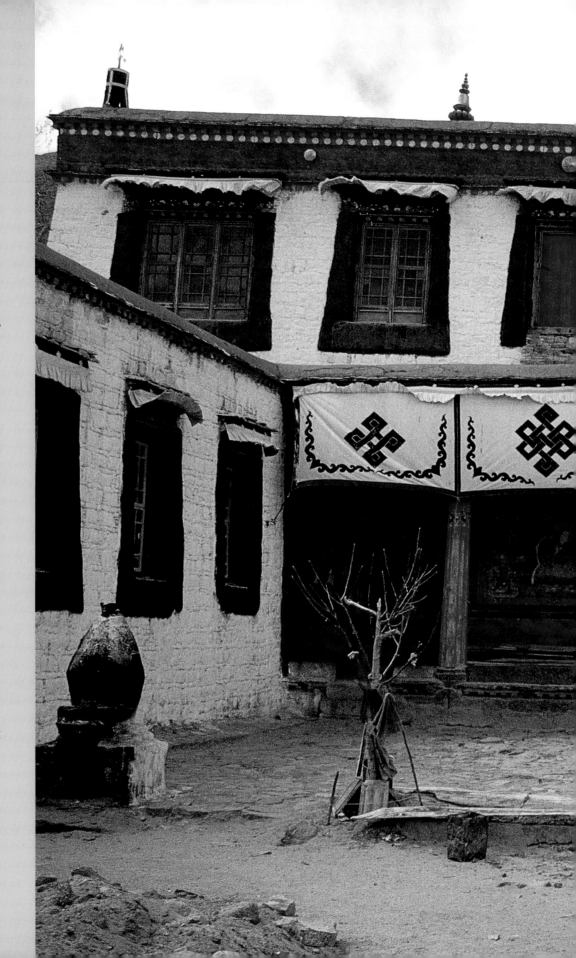

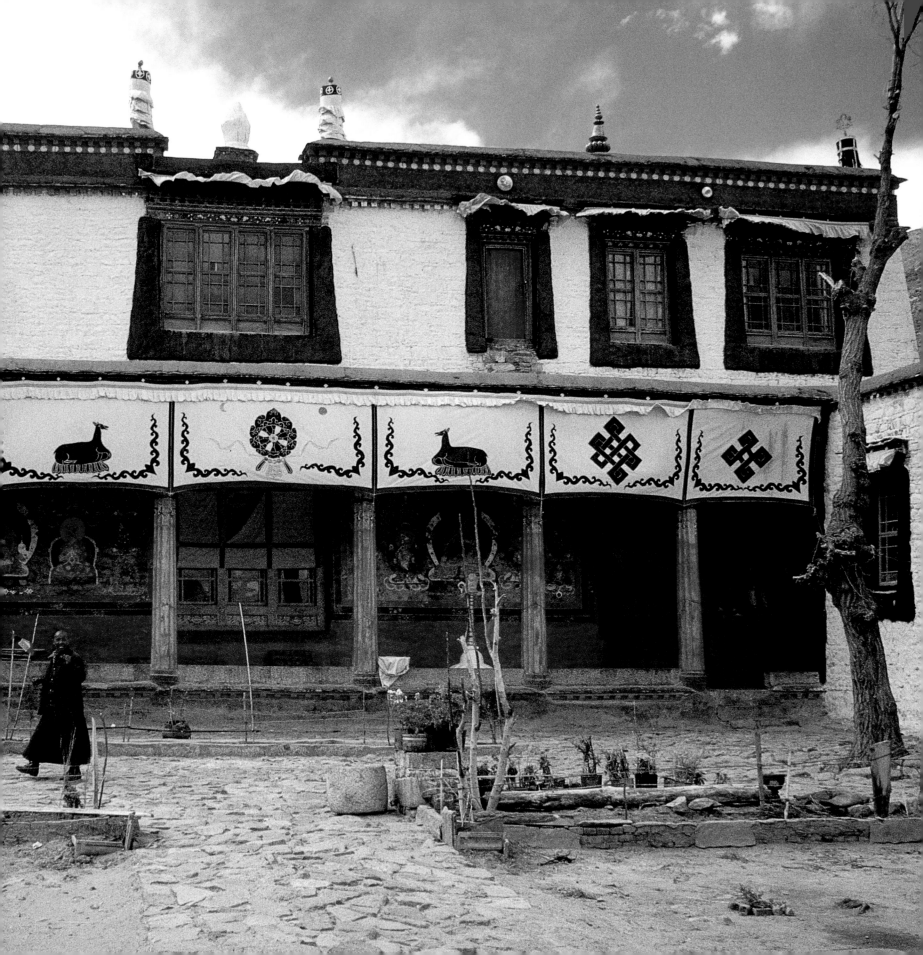

THE TRANSMISSION OF WISDOM

The Buddha did not appoint a successor but rather ordered that his teachings, the *dharma*, should guide the community of his followers after his passing. This led him to establish a precise system for the ordination of monks and the transmission of the *dharma*. Subsequently, the Great Adepts (see page 13) developed spiritual techniques and rituals to enable initiates to acquire superhuman powers and insights, and this necessitated careful procedures of initiation (*sadhanas*). This is because the knowledge of Buddhist scripture, doctrine, and *sadhanas* were considered to be valueless—and indeed dangerous—unless transmitted by a teacher qualified to assess the readiness and spiritual aptitude of potential initiates. The Tibetan word for teacher—*lama*—is a translation of the Sanskrit *guru*.

Spiritual practices received from a *lama* are often described as "esoteric," or "secret," but they are secrets only to the extent that they are disclosed in the right setting at the right time to duly prepared and dedicated students. A key duty of the *lama* is to select the student's special "meditation deity" (*yi-dam*). The *yi-dam* is a protector and divine guarantor, through whom the initiate attains the spiritual powers which lead to the Absolute. The selection of the particular *yi-dam* might be determined by the *lama*'s monastery or school, but it may also involve an assessment of the student's personality. A number of deities—often fierce in nature—preside over human vices, which they can transform into appropriate aspects of wisdom and compassion.

In the course of meditation, the deity might appear in different forms to the initiate. Such divine appearances led to an increase in the number of *sadhanas*, each new variation having its source in a particular vision of a deity experienced by a saint. These variants often found their way into temple wall paintings and *thangkas*.

RIGHT In Tibet, the Buddhist *dharma* was entirely in the hands of teachers, or *lamas*. This painted papier-mâché figure depicts a *lama* wearing the high-pointed cap that is unique to Tibetan Buddhism.

RIGHT Ceremonial helmets of this type are worn by Vajrayana priests. The triple dome of the helmet, surmounted by the prongs of a thunderbolt, are symbols of the higher states of knowledge which result from Tantric initiation and practice.

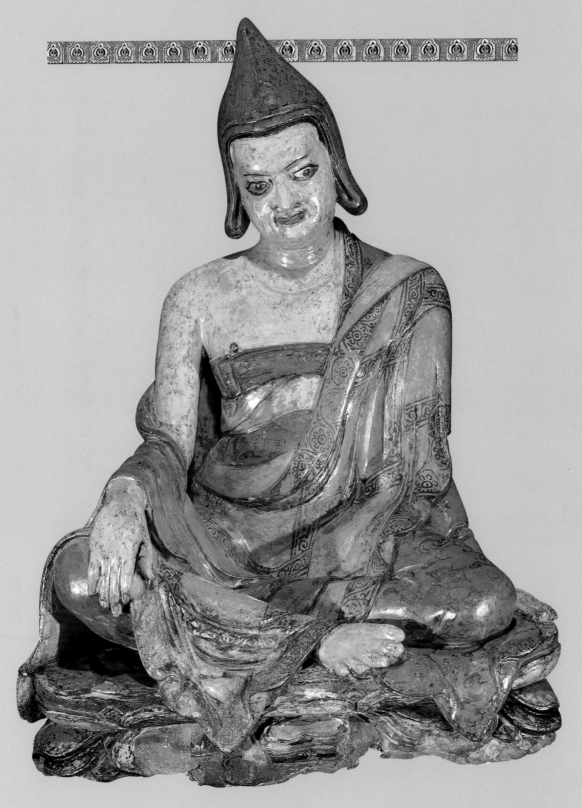

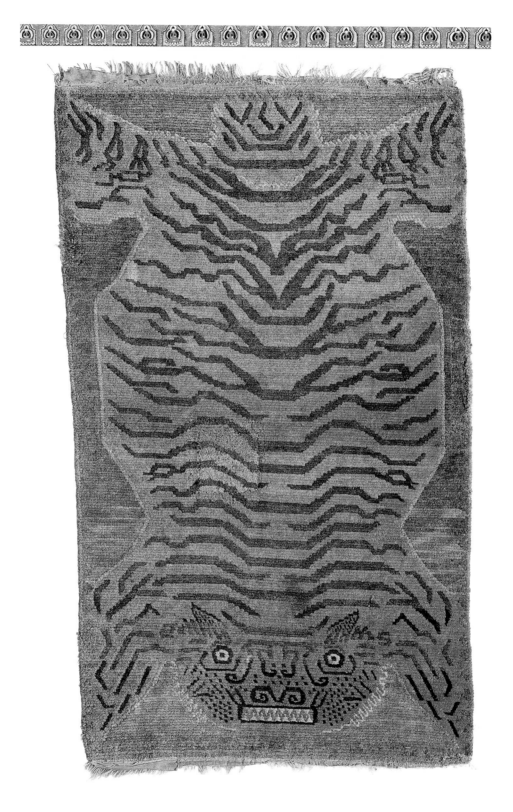

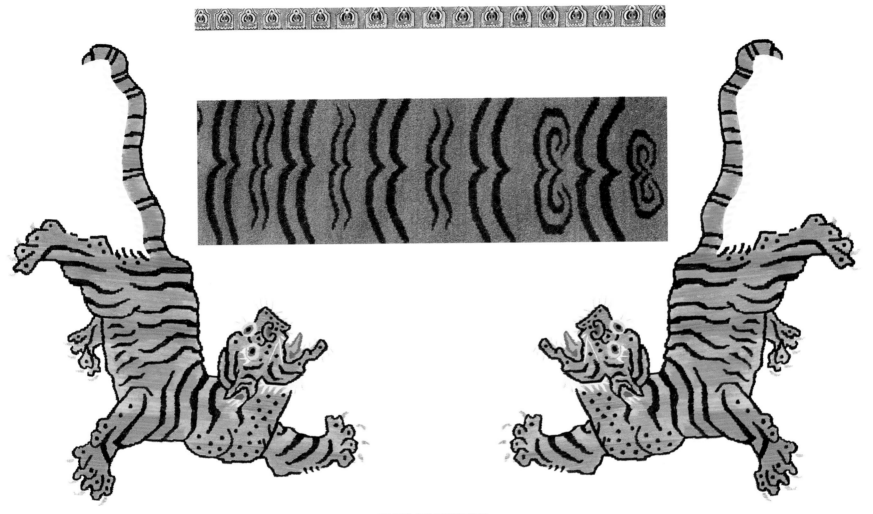

SEATS OF WISDOM

Tibetan tiger rugs owe their popularity to the fact that the Great
Adepts (see page 13) and other high-ranking saints invariably sat on
animal skins to teach and lead rituals. Representing flayed tiger
skins, tiger rugs are among the most unusual designs used by the
carpet weavers of Tibet. The carpet may represent a whole skin—
including the head and claws as illustrated opposite—or the design
may be abstracted and reduced to such an extent that it consists of
simply a repetitive pattern of wavy lines.

COMPASSION INCARNATE

A striking feature of Tibetan Buddhism is the system by which *lama*s reincarnate themselves to secure the succession of their schools and monasteries. The origin of this intentional form of incarnation can perhaps be traced to Padmasambhava, who, with his disciples, is said to sometimes take a human form when hidden texts need to be recovered. Although various *lama*s and schools have made use of reincarnation, it was first deployed over several generations by the Karma-pa school. However, the Sakya-pa hierarchs, who dominated Tibet in the thirteenth century, came to be distinguished instead for their hereditary succession.

The reincarnation system was continued by Gendun Drupa (1391–1474), a disciple of the great scholar and monk Tsong Khapa. Gendun Drupa built up the Gelug-pa order over an exceptionally long and energetic career. Sonam Gyatso (1543–1588), the third head of the Gelug-pa, took the historic step of reestablishing contact with the Mongols, and received the celebrated title Dalai Lama ("Ocean Teacher") when he visited the Mongol leader Altan Khan in 1578. This title was applied retrospectively, so that Gendun Drupa became known as the first Dalai Lama and Sonam Gyatso as the third. The Dalai Lamas are regarded as incarnations of Avalokiteshvara.

Although the Gelug-pa had contacts with Ming China, their powerful position in Tibet was the result of alliances formed with the Mongols. Gushri Khan was deeply impressed by the fifth Dalai Lama (the "Great Fifth"), and with the Khan's military help, the Gelug-pa order established religious and secular hegemony over the whole country, the Dalai Lama becoming the Tibetan head of state.

RIGHT Ngawang Losang Gyatso (1617–1682), the fifth Dalai Lama, was known as the "Great Fifth," on account of his administrative achievements in establishing the Gelug-pa school as the *de facto* rulers of Tibet.

RIGHT The abbots of the Tashilunpo monastery near Shigatse were declared incarnations of Amitabha Buddha by the "Great Fifth" Dalai Lama and became known as the Panchen Lamas ("Great Scholars"). The fifth in the line was Losang Yeshe (1663–1737). In this *thangka*, Amitabha is shown above the head of the Panchen Lama, with Vajra Bhairava, the tutelary deity of the Gelug-pa school, to the left.

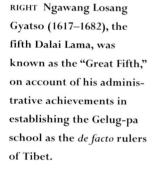

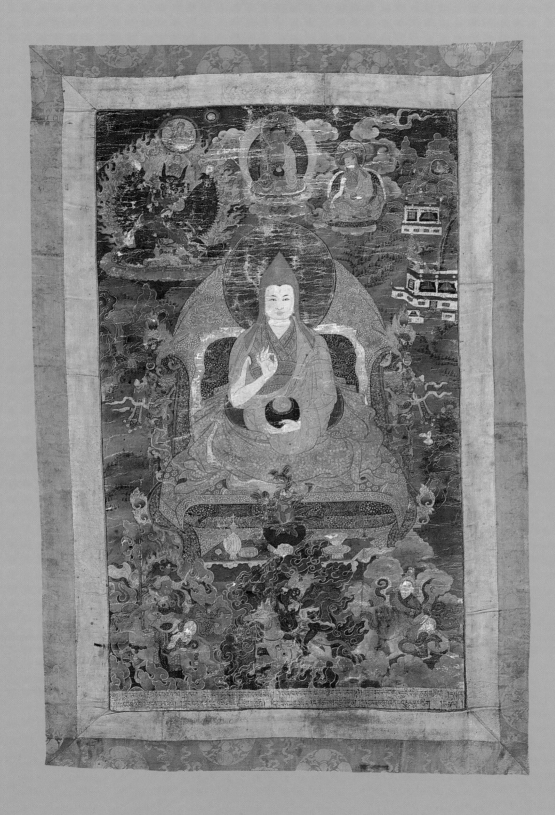

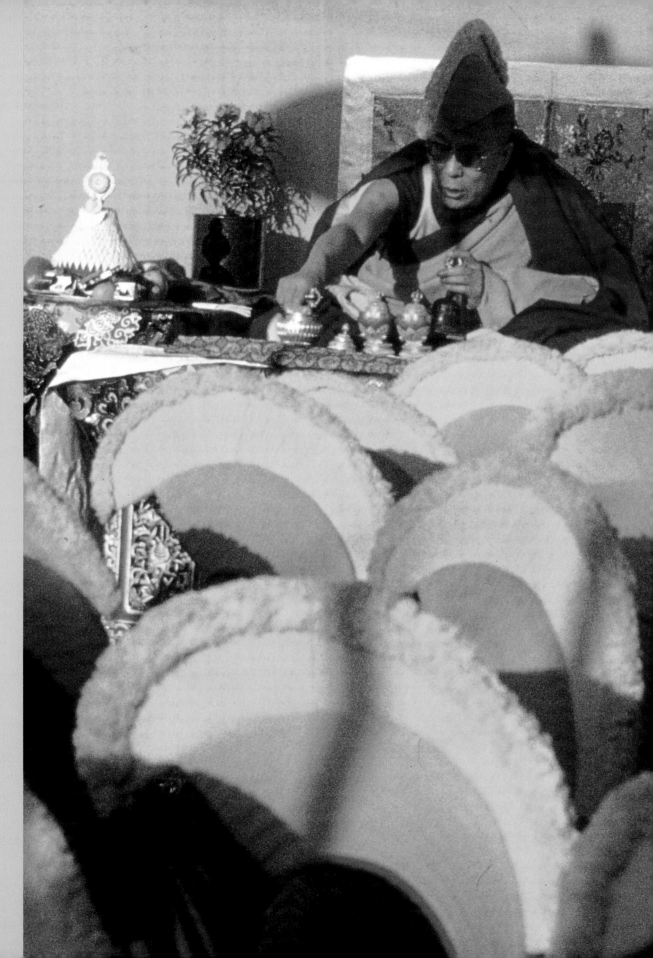

THE PRIEST-KING

When the thirteenth Dalai Lama died in 1933, a search was begun to find his reincarnation. Following ancient practice, the regent, Reting Rinpoche, made a pilgrimage to Lhamo Latso, the "Oracle Lake" in central Tibet. There he had a vision revealing the birthplace of the present Dalai Lama, Tenzin Gyatso, who was born in 1934 to a humble family in the Amdo region of far eastern Tibet. Like other Dalai Lamas, the infant Tenzin Gyatso was taken to Lhasa and educated in seclusion at the Potala Palace.

However, world events were soon to disrupt the life of the young sovereign. After the Communist revolution in China, the Red Army pushed toward Lhasa in 1950 with the aim of "liberating" the country. In 1959, following a popular uprising, the fourteenth Dalai Lama was forced to flee to India, where he established a Tibetan government in exile in Dharamsala. In the security of the Indian Himalayas, he has been able to continue many of the ancient Buddhist traditions of Tibet, such as festivities and prayers to celebrate the New Year, illustrated here. The Dalai Lama and the monks around him are wearing the crested yellow hats of the Gelug-pa school.

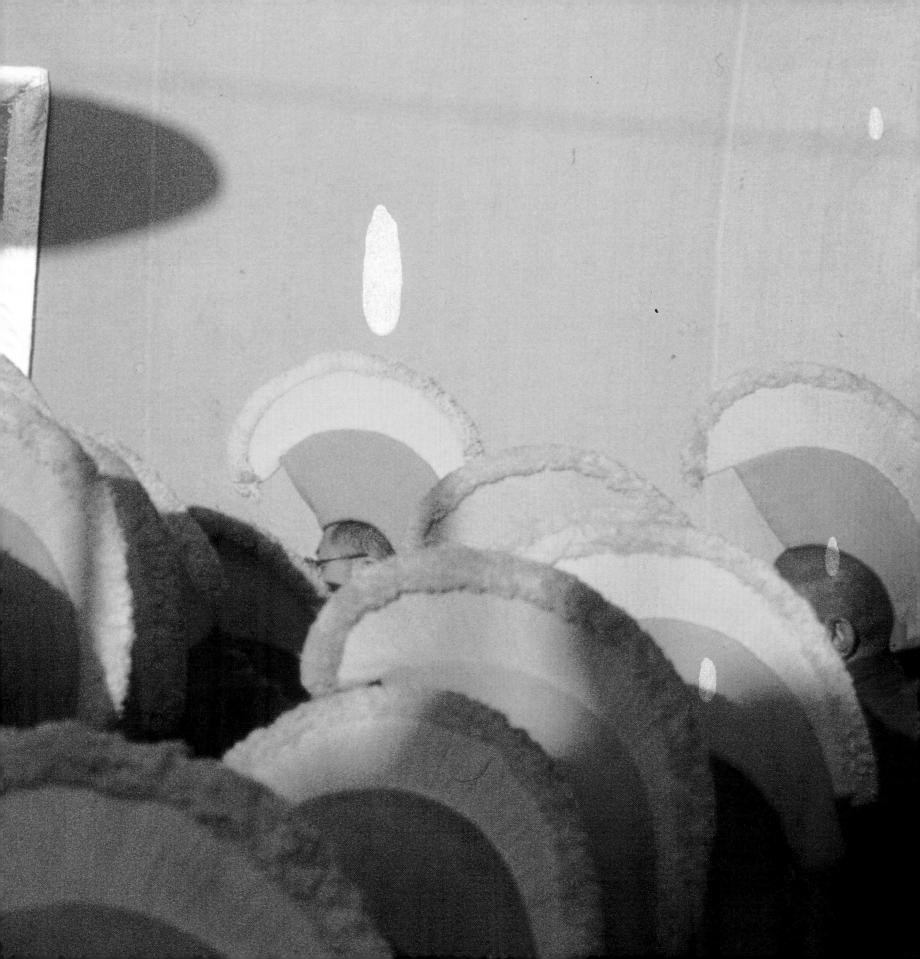

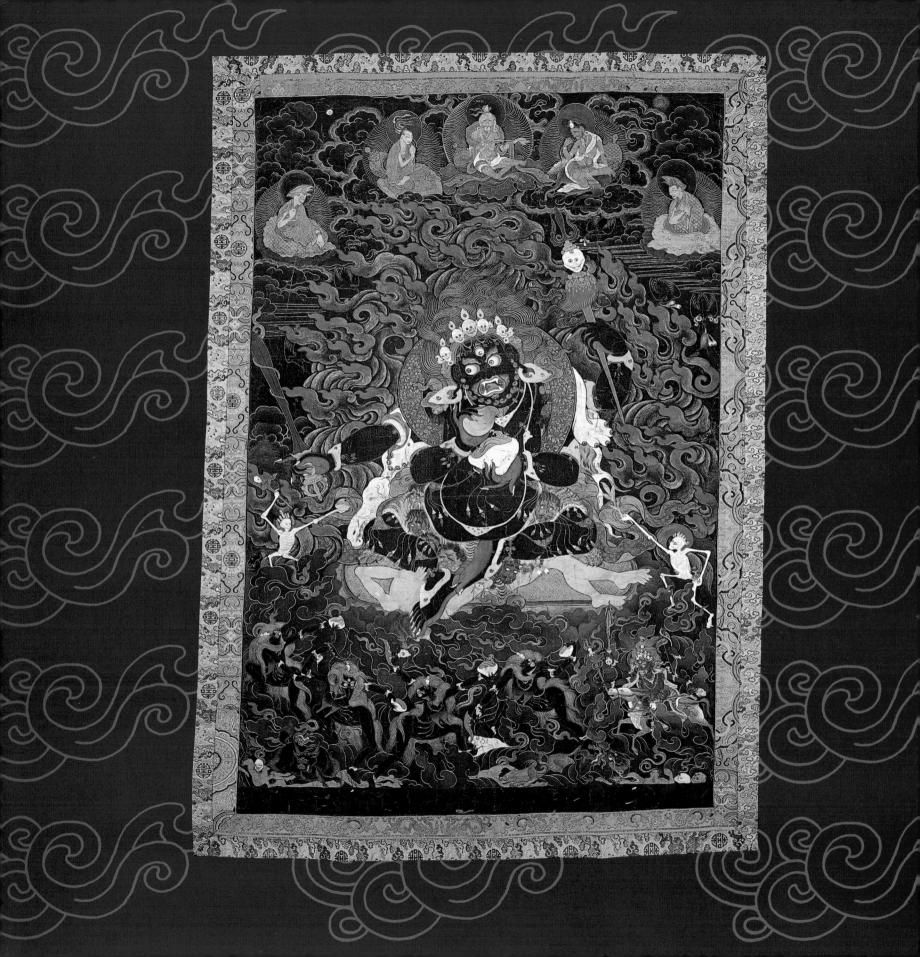

DEITIES FIERCE AND POWERFUL

Many of the gods and goddesses of Tibetan Buddhism appear in a variety of forms, some fierce (*krodha*) and others peaceful (*santa*). This acknowledges the change-able nature of all created things and the underlying reality that the gods represent the moods and features of human consciousness. While most Tibetan Buddhists are drawn to benevolent aspects of the Bodhisattvas and Taras, others choose to meditate on more frightening and dangerous forms. Fierce deities preside over the evil aspects of the personality and their propitiation allows aspirants to confront their own greatest fears and weaknesses. Fierce gods and goddesses are thus channels for grace just as much as their benign counterparts.

LEFT Sarva Buddha Dakini, the "Dakini of all the Buddhas," is depicted wearing an elaborate apron-like necklace inset with turquoise. Displaying the often fierce character of Dakinis (women who have attained supernatural powers), the figure tramples on corpses.

FAR LEFT This *thangka* painting shows the protector deity Maha Kala surrounded by flames and attended by two skeleton spirits. He is seated on a corpse and holds a sword, trident, skull cup, and chopper. Below him are four fierce bird-headed goddesses, and the eques-trian Shri Devi. In the heavens above are *lama*s and *siddha*s, in the center is Saraha (see page 108).

THE TERRIBLE PROTECTORS

The stories which surround the life of the saint Padmasambhava (see page 32) describe him as subduing the ancient pre-Buddhist gods of Tibet with his magical powers, compelling them to watch over the Buddhist faith forever as ferocious Dharma Palas ("Protectors of the *Dharma*"). Although the Protectors have Tibetan aspects, their names suggest that they were originally Indian deities that absorbed local attributes as their cults spread into the Himalayas.

Maha Kala, meaning "Great Time," the most popular of the Dharma Palas, began as a form of the Hindu god Shiva and was believed to embody time, especially time as the inevitable destroyer of all things. In Tibet, Maha Kala functions as a protector of science and a protector of tents. The latter role received special prominence in the sixteenth century when Maha Kala was made the protector deity of Mongolia—a land of tent-dwelling nomads—by the third Dalai Lama.

Yamantaka, whose name means "Destroyer of Death," also holds a unique place among the Dharma Palas. Legends recount that when the god Yama—the Lord of Death—was ravaging the countryside, the people appealed to Manjushri, the Bodhisattva of wisdom. He answered their prayers and assumed the form of Yamantaka, a being so ferocious and powerful that Yama was subjugated and made to serve as a Dharma Pala and Regent of Hell. From the Buddhist perspective, this story represents the abstract truth that eternal wisdom overcomes all ignorance—death being simply an illusion that persists due to a lack of knowledge about the true nature of things. Yamantaka is the tutelary deity of the Gelug-pa school because its founder, Lama Tsong Khapa, is regarded as an incarnation of Manjushri.

RIGHT **In this embroidery, Yama, the Lord of Death, stands on a buffalo mount which tramples on a corpse. Yama is surrounded by flames and holds a noose and skull-crested club.**

RIGHT **This stone stela shows Maha Kala as "Lord of the Tent Pavilion." He holds, in the crooks of his arms, the long wooden sounding board used to summon monks to assembly. This symbolizes Maha Kala's vow to protect all Buddhist monasteries.**

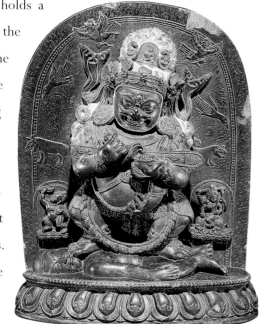

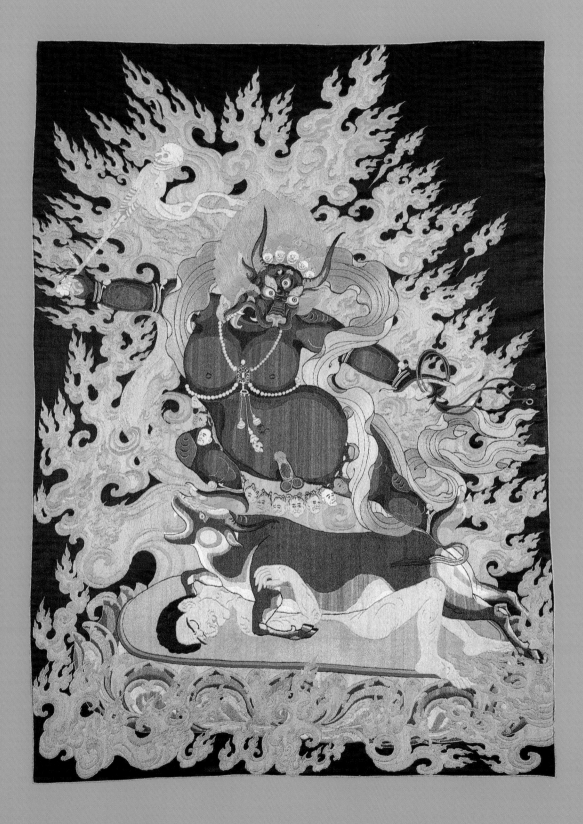

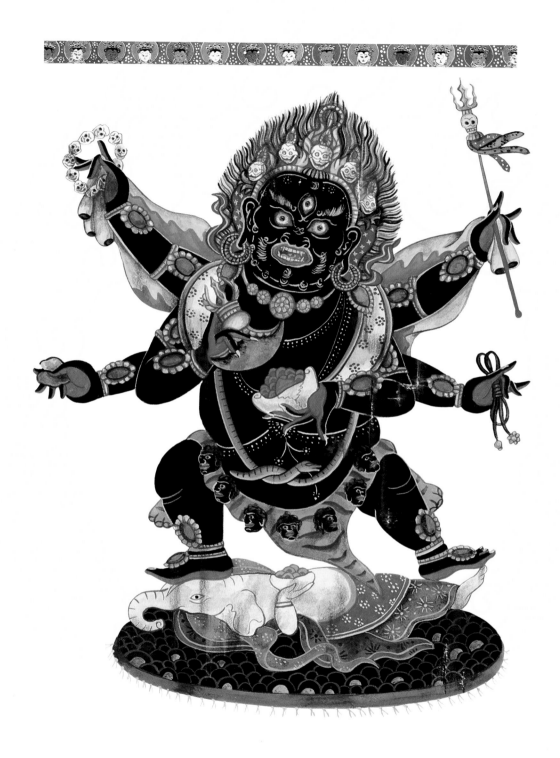

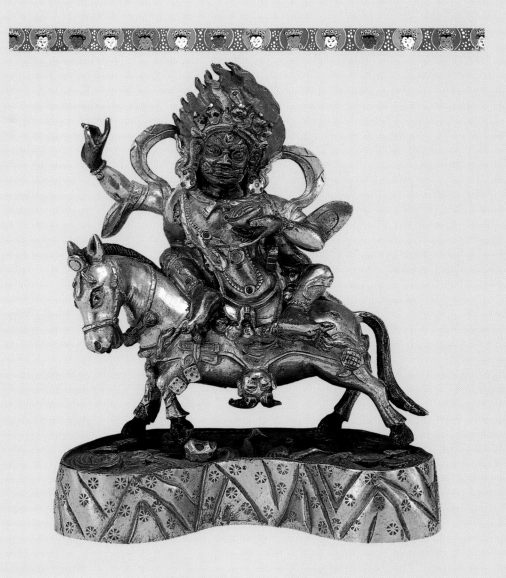

THE GLORIOUS GODDESS

The only female Dharma Pala is Shri Devi, the "Glorious Goddess,"
known as Penden Lhamo in Tibet. She is frequently shown holding a
skull cup filled with blood—as in the gilded, painted bronze figure
above—and riding a mule, draped with the flayed skin of a demon,
across a sea of blood littered with severed limbs. Penden Lhamo
often appears in the retinue of the protector Maha Kala (opposite).

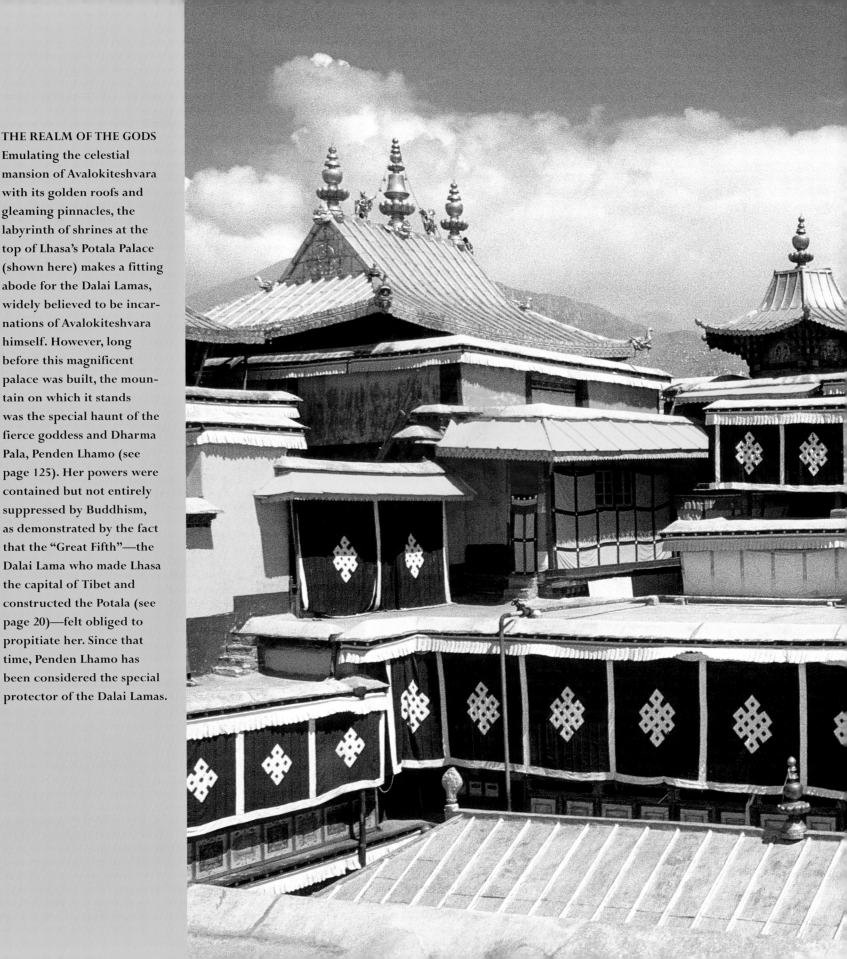

THE REALM OF THE GODS
Emulating the celestial mansion of Avalokiteshvara with its golden roofs and gleaming pinnacles, the labyrinth of shrines at the top of Lhasa's Potala Palace (shown here) makes a fitting abode for the Dalai Lamas, widely believed to be incarnations of Avalokiteshvara himself. However, long before this magnificent palace was built, the mountain on which it stands was the special haunt of the fierce goddess and Dharma Pala, Penden Lhamo (see page 125). Her powers were contained but not entirely suppressed by Buddhism, as demonstrated by the fact that the "Great Fifth"—the Dalai Lama who made Lhasa the capital of Tibet and constructed the Potala (see page 20)—felt obliged to propitiate her. Since that time, Penden Lhamo has been considered the special protector of the Dalai Lamas.

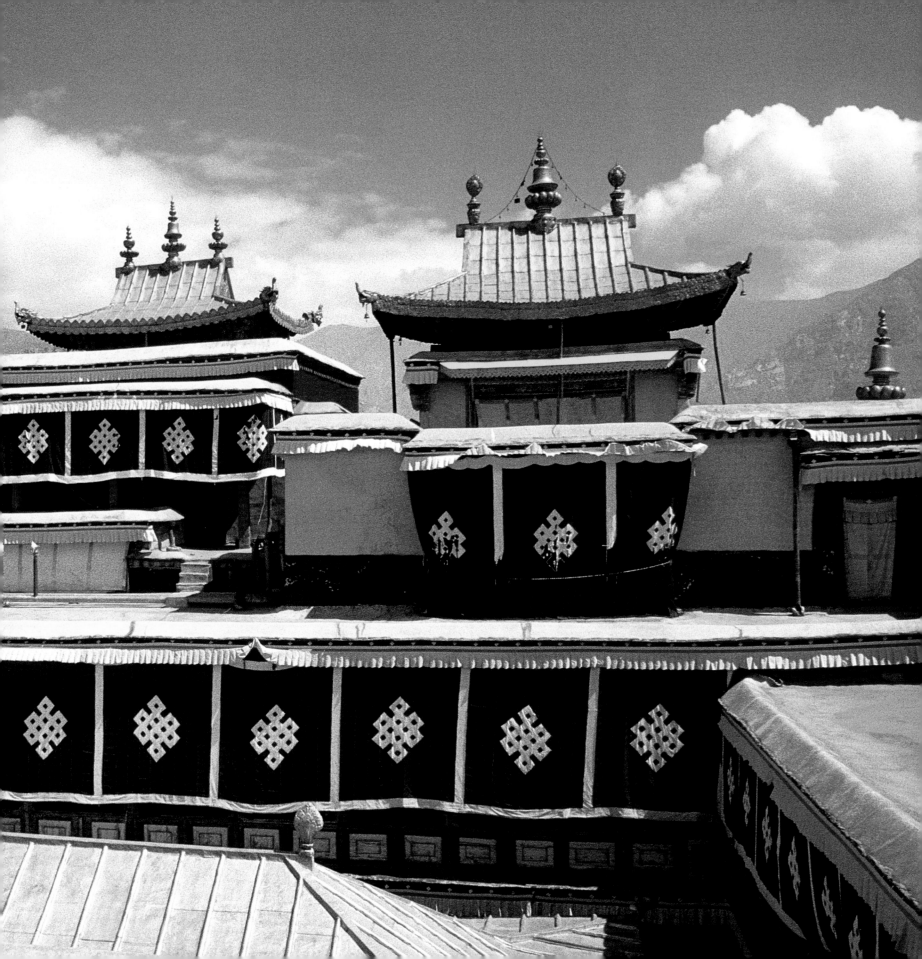

THE CRUEL WANDERERS

BELOW **This ferocious figure of the "Dakini of all the Buddhas" brandishes a curved dagger and holds a skull cup filled with blood.**

There is an old Tibetan belief that all women who acquire supernatural powers become fierce goddesses known as Dakinis. This belief is well illustrated by the story of Ghantapa, a Great Adept (*Mahasiddha*) who is much admired in Tibet. He resided at the monastic university of Nalanda during the ninth century CE, and took the daughter of a local courtesan as his partner and ritual consort. However, because monks are bound by vows of celibacy, these actions caused a public scandal. When confronted for his apparent violation of the monastic rules, Ghantapa and his consort rose into the air, transforming themselves into the deities Chakra Samvara and Vajra Dakini.

Known in Tibetan as *khagro-ma* ("ether wanderers"), the fierce Dakinis are referred to many times in the literature of the Nyingma-pa order, which recounts how they could fly through the air like angels, conveying sages over great distances. As consorts, or "wisdom partners," of the supreme Buddhas, Dakinis have an intimate and firsthand knowledge of special *mantras*, *yoga* practices, and esoteric rites. For this reason, the Great Adepts approached the Dakinis to learn the secret techniques and rituals which could provide them with superhuman insights and incredible powers. Vajra Dakini, also known as Vajra Varahi and Naro Dakini, was considered especially approachable, as she was known for her motherly compassion and nonenvy. Vajra Dakini incarnates herself as the abbess of Samding, the most revered female incarnation in Tibet. The ruins of Samding monastery stand on the edge of Lake Yamdrok, east of Gyantse.

RIGHT **In this statuette of the fierce Karma Dakini, the goddess wears a garland of skulls and sits on a corpse. Dating from the 19th century, it is a companion figure to that shown opposite. Both are carved in wood and painted.**

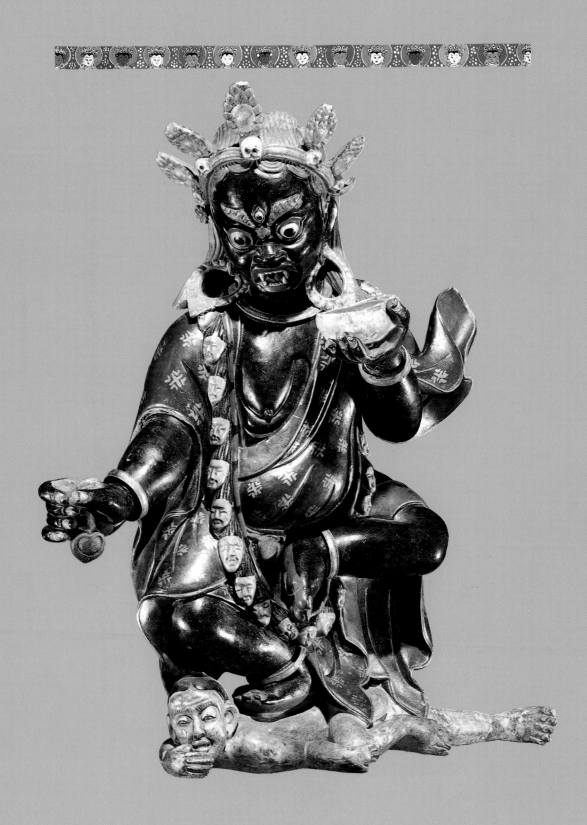

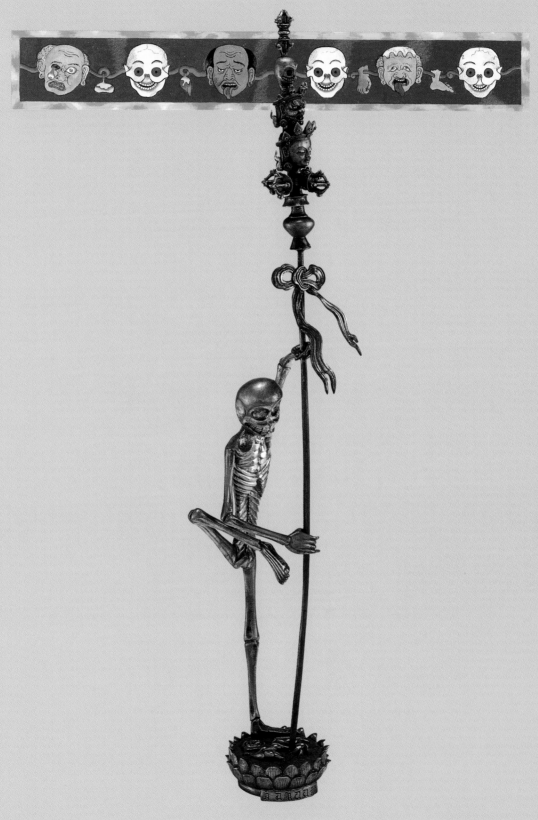

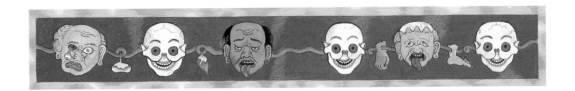

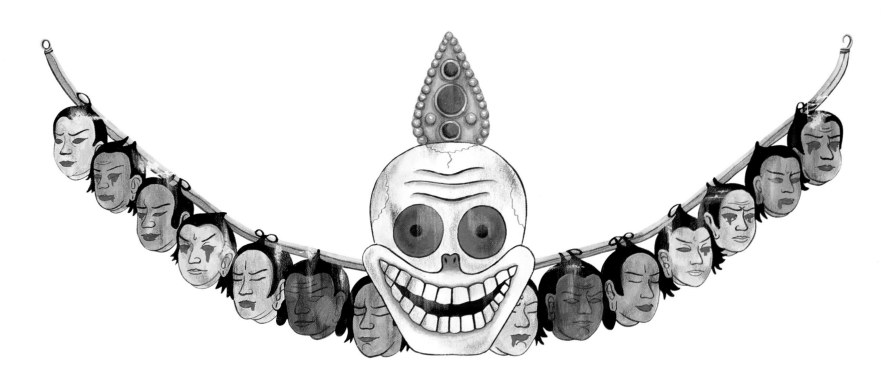

DANCING LORDS OF DEATH

Frightening skeleton beings known as Chiti Patis—literally, "Lords of
the Funeral Pyre"—are one of the unique features of Tibetan art.
Attendants of Yama, the god of death, Chiti Patis are usually shown
dancing and holding thunderbolt standards, as in the example
opposite. The frequent emphasis on death in Tibetan art is not an
indication of a morbid obsession, but rather a reflection of the posi-
tive and pragmatic view that the Tibetan people take of life, and
their belief in the need to appreciate that all existence is transitory.

RITES OF THE CEMETERY

The Tibetans have developed unique ways of disposing of the dead. The most common method is "sky burial," in which the deceased is exposed to the elements, a custom developed due to the scarcity of wood in most parts of the Tibetan plateau. Following Indian practice, eminent *lamas* (spiritual guides) are often cremated and their ashes kept in *chortens* or used in *tsha-tsha* amulets (see pages 58–59). Earth burial, which was used by the ancient kings of the Yarlung dynasty (see page 16), is now reserved for thieves, murderers, and victims of disease.

Although the vital functions may have ceased, individuals are not regarded as truly dead until all consciousness has completely departed. This process is assisted by an officiating *lama*, who performs rituals of "transference" (*pho-wa*) and whispers advice about the successive visions that the deceased will encounter in the afterworld (see page 134). Special prayers and offerings are made which add to the merit of the dead and assure their well-being in the next life.

When these essential religious rites have been performed, the corpse is cut into pieces and taken to a designated charnel ground, usually a hilltop outside the village or town. The sky burial ground shown here—near Hongyuan, in the eastern province of Kham—is not unlike those found throughout Tibet. The remains of the body are left in the open to be eaten by vultures and other animals as a final act of generosity, allowing other beings to be nourished by what has become an otherwise useless residue. Some charnel grounds, including that at Sera in central Tibet, are thought to be especially auspicious; corpses are sometimes brought considerable distances to be disposed of at such sites.

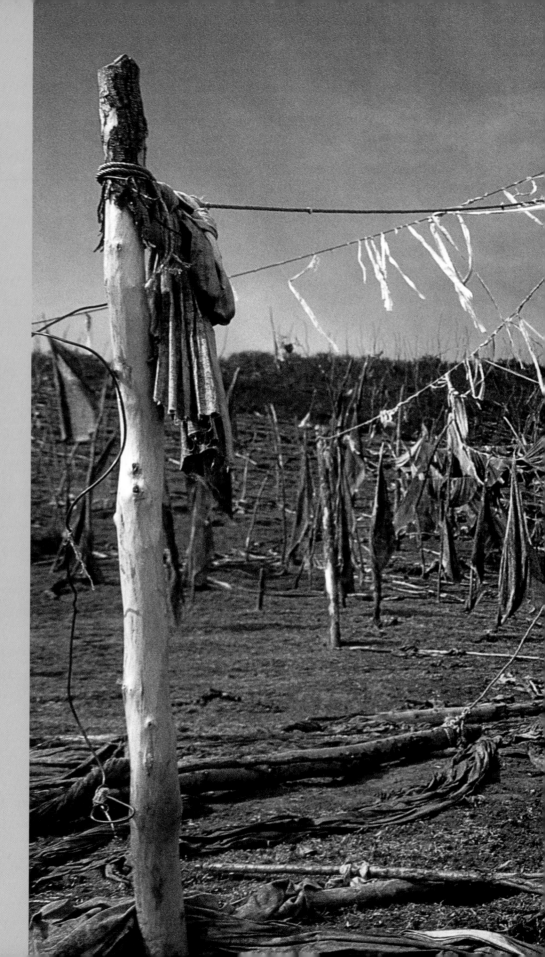

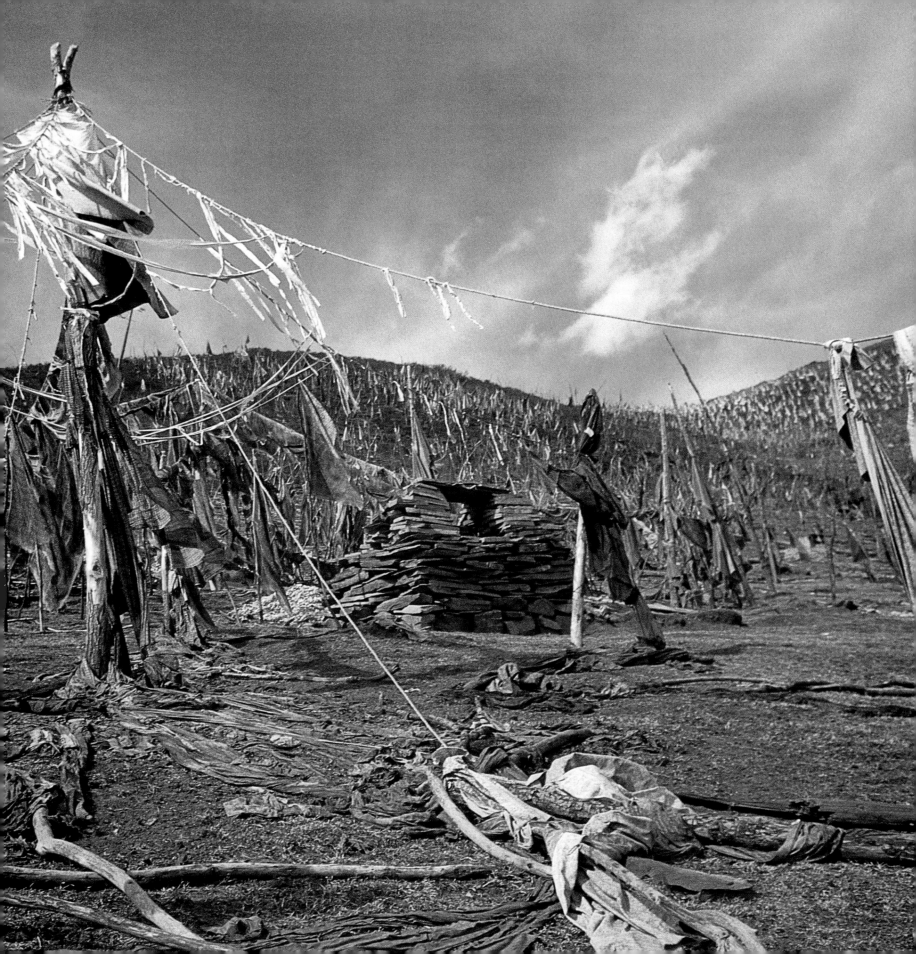

THE WAY THROUGH THE AFTERWORLD

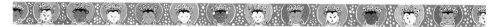

In Buddhism, death is not a final end but merely a gateway to a new reincarnation or—for those who, like the Buddha, are sufficiently prepared—to complete liberation. The period after the death of the physical body is referred to as an "intermediate state" (Tibetan *bardo*), and is described in a number of sources, the most famous of which, dating to around the fourteenth century, is known in the West by the title used by the first translators: *The Tibetan Book of the Dead*.

For Tibetan Buddhists, death and the *bardo* provide an opportunity to rip away the illusions embedded in the physical body and to come face-to-face with reality. This reality is known as the "Buddha-nature." It is latent in all individuals and manifests itself as the peaceful and wrathful deities that are believed to reside in the mind and heart. In the days after death, as an individual's false universe collapses, these deities appear in a succession of powerful visions. Most people, terrified by what they see arising from within themselves, flee toward the comfortable and familiar—attachments that lead them inevitably to rebirth. The good and virtuous souls may be reborn in heaven and the evil may end up in hell. None of these afterworlds is permanent and reincarnation is regarded as inevitable. The pure and heroic, however, are able to look beyond appearances and, taking refuge in the Buddha, they attain complete liberation from the bonds of conditioned existence.

Vajrayana Buddhism re-created the *bardo* through ritual and mental techniques that mimicked the death experience. This was done to prepare individuals for the inevitable and to allow them to reflect on life more clearly.

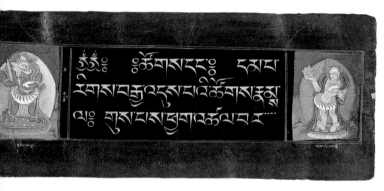

ABOVE **Part of a manuscript of** *The Profound Doctrine of Wisdom's Natural Freedom through Understanding the Intermediate State*, **better known as** *The Tibetan Book of the Dead*. **A** *lama* **would recite the text over the deceased in order to guide him or her through the "intermediate state."**

RIGHT **This** *thangka* **painting illustrates one of the visions experienced in the afterworld. Although horrific, the vision is presided over by Samanta Bhadra, the cosmic Buddha shown at the top of the picture in union with his "wisdom partner."**

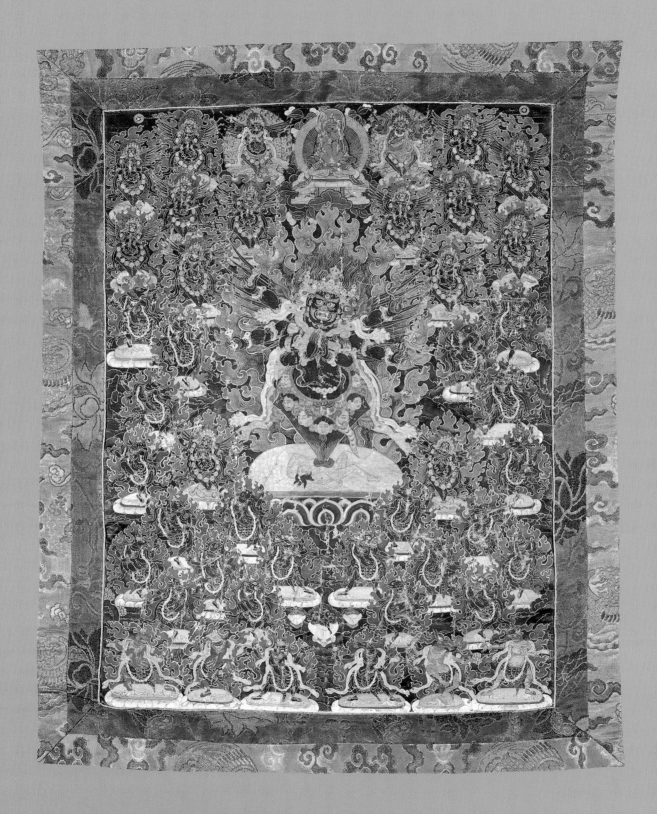

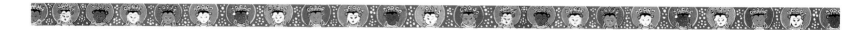

GLOSSARY

Arhat ("Worthy One") A title given to several of the Buddha's early followers who succeeded in attaining *nirvana* (enlightenment).

Bodhisattva ("One Whose Essence is Supreme Knowledge") A divine figure embodying compassion. Bodhisattvas stand on the verge of enlightenment but delay *nirvana* in order to assist others to reach liberation.

Buddha ("One Who Knows") A title given to Siddhartha Gautama or Shakya Muni, the "historical" Buddha (ca. 563–483BCE) and, more generally, to the **cosmic** and celestial Buddhas.

Cosmic Buddha A divine embodiment of supreme knowledge, such as Vajra Sattva ("Diamond Being") and Vajra Dhara ("Holder of the Diamond").

chorten (Sanskrit: *stupa*) A mound of earth, brick, or stone housing Buddhist relics. Tibetan *chortens* may also be metal reliquaries, kept on Buddhist altars.

Dakini A fierce female deity, often portrayed as a female consort, or "wisdom partner," of one of the supreme Buddhas.

Dalai Lama ("Ocean Teacher") The title given to a prominent *lama* of Tibet's Gelug-pa Buddhist order in 1578. The Dalai Lama became Tibet's sacred and secular leader until the exile of the fourteenth Dalai Lama in 1959.

dharma The teachings of the Buddha (often translated as "law" or "truth").

Dharma Pala (*"Dharma* protector") One of numerous pre-Buddhist gods of Tibet, who were subdued by the saint Padmasambhava and subsequently became fierce protectors of the Buddhist faith.

lama (Sanskrit: *guru*) A Tibetan Buddhist teacher or spiritual guide.

Mahasiddha ("Great Adept") A Buddhist adept who gained *nirvana* (enlightenment) by following the "rapid path" of **Vajrayana** and went on to teach the esoteric rites collectively known as Tantra (see page 105).

Mahayana ("Great Vehicle") The tradition of Buddhism that is prevalent in Tibet. According to Mahayana, only after the diligent cultivation of virtue over hundreds of lifetimes can an individual become a **Bodhisattva**.

mandala A map of the Buddhist cosmos, often based on the form of a circle within a square and used as an aid in meditation and the pursuit of *nirvana* (enlightenment). *Mandala*s can take two- or three-dimensional forms.

mantra Spoken or chanted words or phrases repeated in Buddhist worship or meditation. The most popular *mantra* is *Om mani padme hum.*

nirvana ("without desire") Enlightenment, a state of complete nonattachment to the material world. The attainment of *nirvana* is the aim of all Buddhists.

thangka A Tibetan votive painting on a cloth scroll depicting deities, sacred beings, or saints. *Thangka*s are used in worship and meditation.

vajra The pronged thunderbolt that is an emblem of the indestructibility of the Buddhist "final state" of reality, known as *sunyata.*

Vajrayana ("Vehicle of the Diamantine Thunderbolt") A school of Buddhism which asserts that a "rapid path" to *nirvana* (enlightenment) can be found by using special techniques and rituals collectively known as Tantra (see page 105).

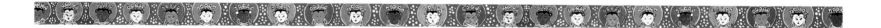

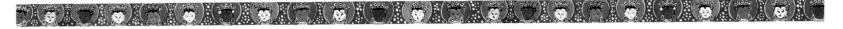

FURTHER READING

Aris, Michael, and Kye, Aung San Suu, eds. *Tibetan Studies in Honour of Hugh Richardson*. Aris and Philips: Warminister, 1980.

Bechert, Heinz, and Gombrich, Richard, eds. *The World of Buddhism: Buddhist Monks and Nuns in Society and Culture*. Thames and Hudson: London, 1984.

Béguin, Gilles. *Art ésotérique de l'Himâlaya*. Réunion des Musées Nationaux: Paris, 1990.

Béguin, Gilles. *Dieux et démons de l'Himâlaya: Art du bouddhisme lamaïque*. Editions des Musées Nationaux: Paris, 1977.

Bhattacharyya, D. C. *Studies in Buddhist Iconography*. Munshiram Manoharlal: New Delhi, 1978.

Bhattacharyya, D. C. *Tantric Buddhist Iconographic Sources*. Munshiram Manoharlal: New Delhi, 1974.

Brauen, Martin. *Das Mandala: Der Heilige Kreis im tantrischen Buddhismus*. DuMont: Cologne, 1992.

Chandra, Lokesh. *Buddhist Iconography*, 2 vols. Aditya Prakashan: New Delhi, 1987.

Chattopadhyaya, Alaka, and Lama Chimpa. *Atisa and Tibet*. Indian Studies Past and Present: Calcutta, 1967.

Clark, Walter Eugene. *Two Lamaistic Pantheons*, Reprint ed. Paragon: New York, 1965.

Dagyab, Loden Sherap. *Tibetan Religious Art*, 2 vols. Harrassowitz: Wiesbaden, 1977.

Dargyay, Eva M. *The Rise of Esoteric Buddhism in Tibet*. Motilal Banarsidass: Delhi, 1977.

Dasgupta, S. B. *An Introduction to Tantric Buddhism*. University of Calcutta: Calcutta, 1950.

Dowman, Keith. *The Power Places of Central Tibet: A Pilgrim's Guide*. Routledge and Kegan Paul: London, 1988.

Essen, Gerd-Wolfgang, and Thingo, T. T. *Padmasambhava*. DuMont: Cologne, 1991.

Goepper, Roger. *Alchi: Ladakh's Hidden Sanctuary, The Sumtsek*. Serindia: London, 1996.

Gordon, A. *The Iconography of Tibetan Lamaism*. Columbia University Press: New York, 1939.

Heruka, Gtsansmyon. *The Life of Marpa the Translator*. Shambala: Boston, 1986.

Huntington, S. L., and Huntington, J. C. *Leaves from the Bodhi Tree*. University of Washington: Seattle, 1990.

Jackson, David. *A History of Tibetan Painting*. Österreichische Akademie der Wissenschaften: Vienna, 1996.

Kvaerne, Per. *An Anthology of Buddhist Tantric Songs*. Universitetsforlaget: Oslo, 1977.

Legshay, Gyatsho. *Gateway to the Temple: Manual of Tibetan Monastic Customs, Art, Building and Celebrations*. Ratna Pustak Bhandar: Kathmandu, 1979.

Lowenstein, Tom. *The Vision of the Buddha*. Duncan Baird Publishers: London, 1996; Little, Brown: New York, 1996.

Reynolds, V., and Heller, A. *Catalogue of the Newark Museum Tibetan Collection*, 2 vols. The Newark Museum: Newark, 1983.

Ricca, Franco, and Lo Bue, Eberto. *The Great Stupa of Gyantse*. Serindia: London, 1993.

Richardson, Hugh. *High Peaks, Pure Earth: Collected Writings on Tibetan History and Culture*. Serindia: London, 1998.

Richardson, Hugh. *Tibet and its History*. Oxford University Press: London, 1962.

Snellgrove, David, and Richardson, Hugh. *A Cultural History of Tibet*. Weidenfeld and Nicolson: London, 1968.

Snellgrove, David. *Indo-Tibetan Buddhism: Indian Buddhists and their Tibetan Successors*, 2 vols. Shambala: Boston, 1987.

Thurman, Robert A. F., trans. *The Tibetan Book of the Dead*. Aquarian: London, 1994.

Tucci, Giuseppe. *Indo-Tibetica*, 4 vols. Reale Accademia d'Italia: Rome, 1932–1941.

Tucci, Giuseppe. *The Religions of Tibet*, translated by Samuel, G. University of California: Berkeley, 1980.

Uhlig, H. *Tantrische Kunst des Buddhismus*. Berlin, 1981.

von Schroeder, Ulrich. *Indo-Tibetan Bronzes*. Visual Dharma Publications: Hong Kong, 1981.

Wayman, Alex. *The Buddhist Tantras: Light on Indo-Tibetan Esotericism*. Kegan Paul: London, 1995.

White, D. G. *The Alchemical Body: Siddha Traditions in Medieval India*. University of Chicago Press: Chicago, 1996.

Zwalf, W. *Heritage of Tibet*. British Museum: London, 1981.

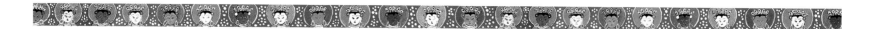

INDEX

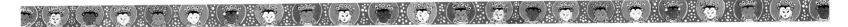

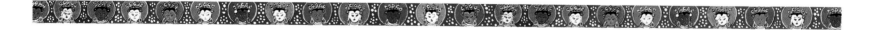

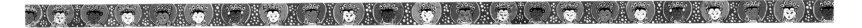

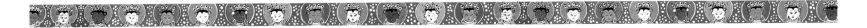

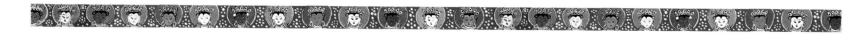

PICTURE CREDITS

The publisher would like to thank the following people, museums, and photographic libraries for permission to reproduce their material. Every care has been taken to trace copyright holders. However, if we have omitted anyone, we apologize and will, if informed, make corrections in any future editions.

Abbreviations

t top; **c** center; **b** bottom; **l** left; **r** right

BAL: Bridgeman Art Library, London/New York

BLOIOC: British Library Oriental and India Office Collections, London

BM: British Museum, London (Oriental Antiquities)

RHPL: Robert Harding Picture Library, London

TI: Tibet Images, London

Cover TI/Ian Cumming; **page 1** Graham Harrison; **2** TI/Ian Cumming; **3** BM (1880-376); **6–7** Magnum Photos/Raghu Rai; **8** TI/Ian Cumming; **9** BM (1913,4-18.2); **10** BM (1880-11); **11** BM (1944,11-13,0.19); **12** BM (1990,4-9.1); **13** BM (1965, 5-25-2); **14–15** RHPL/David Tockeley; **16** RHPL/Sassoon; **18** Julia Hegewald; **19** TI/Stone Routes; **20–21** TI/Ian Cumming; **22** TI/John Miles; **23** TI; **24** BM (1992,12-14.13); **25** Axiom/Chris Bradley; **26** BM (1880-309); **27** BM (1895,2-9.3); **29** BM (1946,10-18.1); **30** BM (1906,7-18.0,13); **31** Julia Hegewald; **32** BM (1942, 4-16.1); **33** TI/Ian Cumming; **34** BM (1939,1-18.1); **35** BM (1939,1-18.1); **36** BAL/Oriental Museum, Durham; **37** BM (1906,12-26.09); **39** BM (1944,4-1.0,5); **40–41** TI/Ian Cumming; **42–43** TI/Ian Cumming; **44** TI/Ian Cumming; **45** BM (1894, 12-13.1); **46** BM (1905,5-19.20); **48** BM (1987,5-20,0.1); **49** TI/Mani Lama; **50** BM (1992,12-14.21); **51** TI/Ian Cumming; **52** Magnum Photos/Raghu Rai; **53** BM (1992,12-14.52); **54–55** Axiom/Jim Holmes; **56** BM (1940,10-5.1); **57** BM (1948, 7-16.22); **58** Julia Hegewald; **59l** BM (1992,12-14.85); **59r** BM (1992,12-14.85); **61** BM (1939,5-17.1); **62** TI/Ian Cumming; **63** BLOIOC (OR 13813); **64** BM (1919-473); **65** TI/Merilyn Thorold; **66** BM (1992,12-14.16); **67** BM (1946,7-13.13 a&b); **68** BM (1895,4-8.24); **69** RHPL/Gavin Hellier; **70–71** Julia Hegewald; **73** BM (1992, 12-14.96a); **74** TI/Ian Cumming; **75** TI/Ian Cumming; **76** BM (1905,5-19.86); **78** BM (1992,12-14.19); **79** TI/Ian Cumming; **80** TI/Ian Cumming; **81** BM (1919, 1-1,0.34); **82–83** BLOIOC (OR 6724, Box 14, Vol 1); **84** BM (1954,2-22.8); **85** BM (1954,2-22.8); **86** BM (1948,7-16.11); **87** BM (1980,12-20,0.11); **89** BM (1893, 3-20.133); **90–91** Royal Geographical Society/Chris Caldicott; **92** BM (1973,5-14.2); **93** BM (1980, 12-20.0.16); **94** BM (1992,12-14.36); **95** BM (1985,3-1.1); **96** BAL/Oriental Museum, Durham; **98** BM (1898,4-8,0.33); **99** BM (1893,30-20.11); **102** BM (W412); **103** BM (1956,12-18.0.12); **104** BM (1957, 4-13,0.1); **105** BM (1956,12-10.6); **106–107** TI/Stephen Batchelor; **108** Art Resource/Newark Museum, New Jersey (49.41); **109** BM (1956,7-14.0.40); **110–11** TI/Stephen Batchelor; **112** BM (1948,7-16.6); **113** BM (1908,5-15.2); **114** Mimi Lipton/Heine Schneebeli; **115** John Eskenazi Ltd; **116** John Bigelow Taylor/Rose Art Museum, Brandeis University, Mass. Gift of N & L Horch to the Riverside Museum Collection; **117** BM (1980,12-20.0.8); **118–119** Magnum Photos/Raghu Rai; **120** BM (1949,11-12,0.1); **121** BM (1921,2-19.3); **122** BM (1908,5-15.10); **123** BM (1961,10-14,0.5); **125** BM (1907,5-24.4); **126–127** Julia Hegewald; **128** BM (1948,7-16.24); **129** BM (1948,7-16.23); **130** BM (1893,3-20.5); **132-133** TI/Catherine Pratt; **134** BLOIOC (OR15190.3 Part 3); **135** BM (1956, 12-8,0.15).